Called to CARE

By James P. Rousey

To Deb, who first suggested that I write a book sixteen years ago and has supported and loved me every day.

All proceeds from the sale of this book will go to the River Foundation, which was established by First Southern to strategically give back to God and to partner with Christian Ministries, locally and globally.

From regular, pre-tax tithing received from the Family of Companies, the River Foundation Donor Advised Fund at the National Christian Foundation invest in Christ-centered ministries in the Commonwealth, the United States and internationally.

Grants are directed toward specific categories that reflect the hearts of our team members and leadership team.

Called to CARE

© 2018 Jim Rousey

ISBN 978-0-9740602-8-6

Chilidog Press, Loveland, Ohio

For information, contact the author:
Jim Rousey
205 N. Depot Street
Stanford, KY 40484
jrousey@utgins.com

Published by:
Chilidog Press LLC
Loveland, Ohio
www.chilidogpress.com

Cover: Josh Bowles
Book design: Andy Melchers
Editorial assistance: Scott Coffman

Table of Contents

Foreword 7

Chapter 1 — Why You Should CARE 9

Chapter 2 — Calling 19

Chapter 3 — Attitude 37

Chapter 4 — Respect 55

Chapter 5 — Excellence 69

Chapter 6 — Care Enough to Dare Enough 85

Thought Conditioners 95

Chapter Discussion Questions 100

Bibliography 105

Note of Thanks 113

Foreword

In•teg•ri•ty (in 'tegrədē): The quality of being honest and having strong moral principles; moral uprightness. The state of being whole and undivided.

Integrity is the reason that *Called to CARE* is such a powerful and practical book. Jimmy Rousey is a man of integrity who lives the compelling principles that he addresses in *Called to CARE*—in his faith, family, business, and friendships.

I know.

As a long-time board member, I've observed how skillfully he leads a company dedicated to succeed in three bottom line measurements: financial, social, and spiritual. As a friend, I've experienced Jimmy's care and concern as my wife and I have walked through a journey dealing with her breast and bone cancer. Jimmy is deeply committed to Christ and to his wife, Debbie.

When Jimmy asked me to read a draft of *Called to CARE*, I expected I would read it once and that it might help me in one or two areas of my life. How wrong I was—the book is dynamite! I will read it again and again because it is packed with truth that is not complex to understand, but is life-changing.

Called to CARE beautifully addresses how to:
- Determine your calling.
- Develop a life-giving attitude and put it into action.
- Learn to respect people and build authentic relationships.
- Become excellent in your work and your entire life.
- Make the most of your time.
- Leave a lasting legacy.

I heartily recommend this book. But I need to warn you: Most likely, you'll read it again and again.

Howard Dayton
Founder of Compass – Finances God's Way

Why You Should CARE

The way of a fool is right in his own eyes,
but he who is wise listens to counsel.[1]

Most people spend much of their lives searching for answers. It always seems that finding the answers to questions is our ultimate goal. That's what many of us learned growing up, right? Give the right answers, get the good grades, and then you will have succeeded.

The problem with that philosophy is that not everything that we learn in school applies to our everyday lives. We can study and cram to learn all the right answers to the questions on our final exams; however, once those final exams are completed, once our graduation tassels are flipped and we enter the "real world," what many of us find is that, although we thought we had learned all the answers, life has changed the questions. Then we have to begin the search for answers all over again.

Plans fail for lack of counsel, but with many advisers
they succeed.[2]

Many people are successful in business as well as other areas without ever having had a formal education or a college degree. So how did these people find success? Robert Half, the founder of employment agency Robert Half International, observed, "Asking the right questions takes as much skill as giving the right answers."[3] The trick is finding the right question.

Ask the right question to the right person,
get the right answer, and make the right decision.

That sounds simple enough, but it doesn't take much practice to learn that it is anything but simple. Indeed, figuring out the right question is usually a much greater mental exercise than answering someone else's question. And even if you do have the right question, to whom do you ask it?

The Book of Proverbs is replete with examples that all seem to have a similar proposition regarding how to obtain wisdom effectively: ask for it. Then ask for it again. Then continue asking for it. You need to exercise some judgment to find the right people to ask. If someone in your life has succeeded in an area where you would like to succeed, then there's a good chance that this person knows something that you need to know. So ask. Find as many people like that as you can, and keep on asking. Eventually, you will learn what you need to know to make the right decision.

However, there is one matter that must be settled first...

What is the question?

It doesn't matter how many answers you receive from however many advisers—if you ask the wrong question, the answers you receive will not lead you to any meaningful decision. So how does one find the right question?

As an example, let's look at the question, "Do you CARE?" It is a question that can only be answered with a "yes" or a "no." Neither an affirmative nor a negative response leads to a decision, however. That indicates that this is not the right question. You could ask any yes/no question to a hundred people and your only accomplishment would be the accumulation of polling statistics. The answers don't lead anywhere.

> So then, my dearest friends, as you have always followed my advice—and that not only when I was present to give it—so now that I am far away be keener than ever to work out the salvation that God has given you with a proper sense of awe and responsibility. For it is God who is at work within you, giving you the will and the power to achieve his purpose.[4]

Arguably, the most common question to all of humanity is the question of purpose. Why are we here? What are we supposed to be doing? This common quest for purpose rose dramatically to the surface of our culture with the publication of Rick Warren's 2002 book, *The Purpose Driven Life*, which has recently been re-released for a new generation with the reworked title *What on Earth Am I Here For?* The fact that the book has sold over 32 million copies and has been translated into over fifty languages is ample evidence that this is a universal question.[5]

The answers to the questions, "Why am I here?" and "What am I supposed to be doing?" are going to be unique for every individual on this earth. In the Bible, though, we can find some universal answers to the question of what we are NOT supposed to be doing:

1. Building a personal legacy. It is natural for us to want recognition for our efforts and achievements in the here and now, as well as to have our name and our association with those achievements recorded for posterity. This is why buildings and monuments have people's names on them, usually because money has been donated, or perhaps in honor of a person's philanthropy or fame in the community. However, we are not here to have our own names remembered. Genesis 11:4 records that the motivation for the builders of the Tower of Babel was not so much to reach the heavens, but to make a name for themselves by building it. We all know how that turned out.

2. Pursuing happiness. Yes, the Declaration of Independence lists "the pursuit of happiness" as an unalienable right with which we have been endowed by our Creator. But it doesn't say that personal happiness should be our primary pursuit. Everybody likes to be happy, but living for our own happiness and pleasure is extremely selfish, because the more focused we are on pursuing our own happiness, the less attentive we are to the needs of others. Paul explains it in this way:

It should not be important whether you are sad or whether you are happy. If you buy something, it should not matter to you that you own it. You should use the things of the world without letting them become important to you. This is how you should live, because this world, the way it is now, will soon be gone.[6]

3. Accumulating material wealth for ourselves. This goes hand in hand with the first two. If we were interested in being successful in the world's eyes, then having all the trinkets and trappings of material success would be evident. If we are pursuing happiness as a primary objective, we will be seeking short-term vehicles to transport us to that happy place. This usually means "stuff." To get more stuff, you need more money. To get more money, you need to climb the corporate ladder. To climb the corporate ladder, you need ambition. To muster that level of ambition, you must be self-centered, which takes your eye off the things and people that matter the most. As Paul instructed Timothy:

Warn the rich people of this world not to be proud or to trust in wealth that is easily lost. Tell them to have faith in God, who is rich and blesses us with everything we need to enjoy life. Instruct them to do as many good deeds as they can and to help everyone. Remind the rich to be generous and share what they have. This will lay a solid foundation for the future, so that they will know what true life is like.[7]

So what is this "true life?" What does it mean to have truly succeeded? The world loves to define success as your net worth or the size of your house or how many cars you have. If I became a doctor and healed lots of people, *and* made a lot of money doing it, would that be success? Or what if I became a farmer, had a wife and a couple of kids, never had a lot of money but paid all my bills on time, loved the Lord and had a good reputation in my small farming community? We have a hard time defining what success is because different people in different situations will answer that question differently. This shows us that "What is success?" is the wrong question. Perhaps some better questions would be:

• What is it that motivates us?
• What is our passion?
• What is it that we've done in our lives that has made us feel good about ourselves? And if that's really important to us, then why aren't we doing more of it?

When you stop chasing the wrong things, you give the right ones a chance to catch up to you!

When you ask seniors what they would do differently if they could live their lives over again, they tend to give variations of three responses: they would reflect more, they would risk more, and they would do more that would last beyond their lifetimes. If that's what so many older people wish they had done, why aren't we taking heed and trying to live that way now?

Stop the erosion

The company I represent has on its board of directors two gentlemen who are 86 years old. They are great men who have given us sound advice. One of them came to our meeting recently and said, "Guys, it's time for me to resign. I'm 86 years old. I can't drive here anymore; my son has to drive me. I just don't need to be doing this anymore."

So we honored him at dinner that night, and the next day at the board meeting I said, "We're going to have a meeting, but the last thirty minutes we're going to turn it over to these two men and let them just give us some wisdom. Share with us what you would like us to hear."

The man who was resigning said, "I'm the last living connection to my parents and my grandparents for my children and my grandchildren. My advice to you all is to do everything you can to stop the erosion. I see it today in our society. I see it today in my own family. I see the erosion from my grandparents to me. I see it from me to my grandchildren and beyond. Stop the erosion."

So watch what you do! Be careful with your very life! Don't forget the things you saw with your own eyes, and don't let them fade from your memory. Remember them your whole life; teach them to your children and your grandchildren.[8]

That's how families came to know God back in the Old Testament days. They listened, they learned, and they passed it on.
They didn't have Facebook, email, family photo albums, or an abundance of books. Moses was telling them that their highest priority was to do whatever they could to stop the erosion from generation to generation.

From that perspective, it becomes clearer that the question we need to be considering is not, "Do you care?" so much as it is, "What do you care about?" If someone asked you that question right now, you would probably feel compelled to make a list of the noblest causes or institutions that you could think of. Perhaps you would list God and family first. Maybe your work would be next. Then you might move on to social justice causes such as the poor, the hungry, the homeless, single mothers, orphans, and the elderly.

It's a good thing to have a list of causes like that, but here's the problem: MOST people have a list like that, but their actions do not reflect these values. It's one thing to care about a cause; it's quite another to DO something about it.

Imagine a brother or sister who is naked and never has enough food to eat. If one of you said, "Go in peace; stay warm and have a nice meal!" What good is it if you don't actually give them what their body needs? In the same way, faith is dead when it doesn't result in faithful activity.[9]

When we make a decision to do something, we naturally want to complete our task with excellence. Nobody likes to be on the receiving end of a lousy, half-hearted job. Hopefully, then, we should care enough about the quality of our own work to give our best. Doing so shows respect—for our employers, for our families, for ourselves, but mostly respect for our God who gave us His best by sending His Son, Jesus, to be our greatest example of excellence.

Working with excellence also shows respect for those who advised you to start your venture in the first place. You showed respect to them first by asking them for advice, but it displays even more respect when you act on their advice. To show this respect requires having the proper attitude—both an attitude of openness to receive the advice as well as an attitude of availability to be able to put it into action.

But attitude, respect, and excellence are all pointless without a motivating force: a calling. You must be *Called to Care*.
If a man says that he really cares about his family, but he spends his time and his money in a bar, or gambling, or is unfaithful to his wife, does he really care?

If the leader of a company says he cares about his company, or the staff of his company, does he really live that out? Does he know when the people that work for him, or with him, are struggling? Does he show them he cares? Does he help them out?

If you are serious about not just finding, but LIVING your calling, then being really honest about the answers to certain questions is very, very important—questions that might make you uncomfortable.

Questions such as:

- If you looked at how you spend your time, what does that say you CARE about?

- If you looked at your checkbook, what does that say you CARE about?

- If someone talked to your best friends, what would they say you CARE about?

- If someone talked to your spouse, what would he or she say you CARE about?

- When was the last time you showed someone you CARED, without expecting anything in return?

- Does the way that you live show that you CARE about God?

- Does the way that you live show that you CARE about the things entrusted to you?

If you're like most people, some of your answers to these questions might embarrass you.

At the very least, they probably did not match up with the first things that came to your mind when you first considered the question, "What do you CARE about?" Instead of all those noble causes on your list, your answers might have indicated that you care more about things such as social networking, entertainment, selfish ambition, recognition, comfort, image, or simply getting your own way.

The good news is that with God's help, you can change. The first step in solving a problem is to identify the problem, which is what you just did. The next step is to train yourself to focus on the solution instead of the problem.

Time, Talent, Treasure, and Touch

Management expert Ken Blanchard and S. Truett Cathy, the founder of Chick-fil-A restaurants, wrote a book called *The Generosity Factor*,[10] which tells the story of a young up-and-comer who meets with a company CEO in an effort to learn the secrets of his success. To his surprise, the executive shows the young man that success is defined by how we find ways to give our time, our talents, and our treasure to those in need. This philosophy echoes Jesus' words from the Sermon on the Mount:

> *Do not store up for yourselves wealth here on earth, where moths and rust destroy, and burglars break in and steal. Instead, store up for yourselves wealth in heaven, where neither moth nor rust destroys, and burglars do not break in or steal. For where your wealth is, there your heart will be also.*[11]

To the "Three T's" of time, talent and treasure, I would add a fourth: touch. I remember that before I went on my first mission trip, I did not want to go. I was scared to death of it. For four or five years I had thought about going, but kept putting it off. Then I finally went, and it changed my life. Since then, I've been blessed to be able to take others on mission trips who have never been, and I've watched the trips have an impact on their lives.

A few years ago, I went to Kenya. In Nairobi, I visited Kawangware, one of the largest slums in Africa, where more than three hundred thousand people live on less than a dollar a day.

Before I left on my trip, my truck was approaching a hundred thousand miles. I'd bought it brand new and taken perfect care of it. I started thinking, "A hundred thousand miles. . . I ought to trade in my truck. I could use a new one."

After seeing all those people in Nairobi who had nothing, I decided I didn't need a new truck. I've come to realize that if you own a car, you're in the top 8 percent of the world's population. I had a really good vehicle. Did I really need a new one? Or did I need to show people over in Kenya that I cared about them by helping them?

What did I care about? Did I care about myself, or did I care about them? I spent my *time* going over. I spent what little *talent* I have being there with them. By not spending the money on a new truck,

I could send more *treasure* back. And the reason I was convinced I should do that was because visiting Kawangware made the residents' basic needs personal; I reached out and *touched* them.

And they touched me.

Do not love this world nor the things it offers you, for when you love the world, you do not have the love of the Father in you. For the world offers only a craving for physical pleasure, a craving for everything we see, and pride in our achievements and possessions. These are not from the Father, but are from this world. And this world is fading away, along with everything that people crave. But anyone who does what pleases God will live forever.[12]

We have our own ideas of what's good in life, but many times, these ideas come not from God but from our own passions and cravings. When we focus on those "good" things, we can miss out on God's best for our lives. Some of the things we focus on—our personal appearance, our houses, our possessions—let the world come in and damage our future by distracting us from finding our true calling.

For this reason, the critical question to answer first is, "What do I really CARE about?" Once you've answered that, the next step is to form a plan to do something about it.

It is important to understand that this is a journey. You're not going to read this book and magically come out with all the answers. It might take years before you completely figure out your calling and your plan of action. But, as author and motivational speaker Earnie Larsen once said, "If nothing changes, nothing changes."[13]

So let's get started!

CARE

CALLING

I grew up in a very small town, going to a nice, tiny Southern Baptist Church. My parents had me in church about every time the door was open, and I had no problem with that. When I was 6 years old, I learned that one of my best friends was going to move away. His father was the pastor and he had been "called" to another church. I didn't really understand what that meant, and it bothered me.

After he was gone, our church had an interim pastor, and then they started looking for another pastor to be "called" to come. As a small boy, all I really cared about was if he had any kids, and if he did, that one would be my age, so I could have a new friend.

But I also found it interesting that well into my teenage years and even into the beginning of my young adult years, it seemed like every time I heard about a pastor accepting a "calling" to a new church, the new place was always bigger, and the pastor was always getting more money. In my spiritual walk, that has bothered me a bit.

I'm proud to say now that I can name four pastors I have known who have moved to other churches that were not bigger, and compensation was never even discussed. They weren't running from something, either. These were great pastors who could have stayed where they were. But God was telling them to go somewhere else, and they followed.

For a long time, I thought that a calling was only something that a minister accepted. But what I've come to understand is that we all have a calling.

What is your calling?

Every day is a bank account,
And time is our currency.
So no one's rich, nobody's poor.
We get twenty-four hours each.
So how are you gonna spend?
Will you invest or squander?
Try to get ahead,
Or help someone who's under?
Teach us to count the days.
Teach us to make the days count.
Lead us in better ways.
Somehow our souls forgot Life means so much.[14]

Suppose someone were to give you $1,440 at the beginning of every day for the rest of your life. The only catch is that if you have any of it left at the end of the day, you have to give it back. What would you do? Your first instinct would probably be to spend it, because you wouldn't be able to keep any of it for yourself. Before too long, though, you'd run out of things to spend it on. You can only have so much stuff. So, chances are you'd start looking outside yourself to see what else you could do with that money.

The thing is, all of us already have this in our lives right now, but it's not $1,440 we get to spend. It's 1,440 minutes. We all have the same amount of time at the beginning of the day, and it's all gone at the end. The question is: what are we going to do with the time we have? This question answers itself when we ask ourselves: What do we really CARE about?

The days are long, but the years are short.[15]

There are things in all our lives that we wish we had done differently. None of us would have to take much time to come up with a list of do-overs that we would love to have. Regrets tend to have a common thread: something wasted. Pretty much every "I wish I would've" in our lives falls into one of these four categories:

1. Wasted money: No sooner do we get our first allowance, our first birthday card with money inside, or our first payment for mowing a lawn, than we hear our parents say, "You didn't waste your money on *that*, did you?" Of course, that album, energy drink, or magazine didn't seem like a waste at the time. It was your money; you earned it. So why not spend it on what you want?

But what usually happened next? You would see something else that you wanted, maybe something slightly more valuable or longer-lasting, except now you didn't have the money, because you'd already spent it on a video game you've now beaten three times and are bored with. As a child, this is just one of many fleeting disappointments, and then you're on to the next thing. As an adult, however, this can become a rather unhealthy pattern.

Consider Oskar Schindler, the German industrialist and factory owner who saved the lives of over twelve hundred Polish Jews from extermination in Nazi concentration camps during World War II. Despite the humanitarian effort for which he is best known, he lived extravagantly during the early part of the war. His regret over the ultimate cost of this lifestyle is depicted in a scene from Steven Spielberg's Oscar-winning film, *Schindler's List*:

Oskar Schindler: "I could have got more out. I could have got more. I don't know. If I'd just... I could have got more."

Itzhak Stern: "Oskar, there are eleven hundred people who are alive because of you. Look at them."

Oskar Schindler: "If I'd made more money... I threw away so much money. You have no idea. If I'd just—"

Itzhak Stern: "There will be generations because of what you did."

Oskar Schindler: "I didn't do enough!"

Itzhak Stern: "You did so much."

Oskar Schindler: [Looks at his car.] "This car. Goethe would have bought this car. Why did I keep the car? Ten people right there. Ten people. Ten more people. [Removing Nazi pin from lapel.] This pin. Two people. This is gold. Two more people. He would have given me two for it, at least one. One more person. A person, Stern. For this. [sobbing] I could have gotten one more person... and I didn't! And I... I didn't!"[16]

2. Wasted time: Can I get an "amen" on this one? Who among us is not guilty of letting time slip away from us? What makes us particularly vulnerable to wasting time in 21st Century America is the sheer volume of options that we have to waste it, coupled with what Aldous Huxley called, "Man's almost infinite appetite for distractions."[17]

It seems that our culture is consumed by a craving for shallow, trivial entertainment.

With the advent of television, our entire population developed the habit of stopping whatever we are doing to sit around a glowing box with rapidly moving pictures on it. It didn't take long for families to begin planning their lives around what time their favorite program came on. Have you ever wondered why they're called "programs?" It appears that "programming" is exactly what TV has done to us.

But for some, simply sitting back to watch television wasn't enough. They wanted something more interactive. So the world gave us home video game systems. From the days of *Pong* and *Breakout* to today's game systems that feature movie-like realism, the video gaming market has mushroomed into a $91 billion worldwide industry, according to a 2016 report from market researcher SuperData Research.

But "vegging out" in front of a mindless video game can lose its luster. After all, what can you really learn from shooting holes in a gazillion zombies or moving thousands of brightly colored blocks? No, our liquefying brains needed stimulating, captivating INFORMATION! And thus, the internet was born—the Information Superhighway, where anything you could possibly want to know was just a browser click away.

We browsed, and we browsed, and we browsed some more. Then one day we discovered that we had completely lost our ability to socialize. Instead of talking to friends, we now "interfaced" with our computers. Since no technology can ever replace our inherent need for human contact, we wanted a way to make the internet more personable, more "social" if you will. So they gave us Facebook. In March 2017, there were 1.28 billion people who used Facebook daily.[18] If all of this wasn't enough, now you can do all the above anywhere in the world on your smartphone, so that you never have to miss an opportunity to amuse yourself to death.

According to figures collected by Locket, an Android app, average users check their smartphones 110 times a day. A study by Kleiner, Perkins, Caufield, and Byers estimated a total of closer to 150 times a day.[19] As actor Bill Murray observed, "Phones get thinner and smarter. People get fatter and more stupid."[20]

Remember the 1,440 minutes we all get at the beginning of every day? If you combine the average amount of time that the average American spends watching television,[21] playing video games,[22] surfing the internet,[23] and reading posts on social networks,[24] there goes 384 of those precious 1,440 minutes. If you get eight hours of sleep a night, this means that a full 40 percent of your waking hours are devoted to unadulterated media saturation. Kind of makes you want to think twice before telling somebody you didn't have time to get something done, doesn't it?

3. Wasted worship: When we hear the word "worship," naturally the first thing we think of is God or church. Those of us who are musically inclined might think of hymns or praise songs. But there is much more to the concept of worship than that.

The word "worship" is a shortening of the Old English word *weorthscipe*, from which we also get the word "worthy." To worship is to acknowledge something or someone as being worthy of your attention or affection. For Christians, God obviously fits into that category, but what else does? Worship is our natural response to whatever we value most. Sometimes what our mouths say we value and what our actions show we value are not the same thing. Pastor and public speaker Louie Giglio puts it this way:

"How do you know where and what you worship? It's easy. You simply follow the trail of your time, your affection, your energy, your money, and your loyalty. At the end of that trail you'll find a throne; and whatever, or whomever, is on that throne is what's of highest value to you. On that throne is what you worship."[25]

Whatever is on that throne is what we truly CARE about. If that thing, whatever it is, stands in the way of us fulfilling our calling, then we are worshipping the wrong things.

4. Wasted opportunity: The first three regrets can be summed up in this one. If we squander our money, mismanage our time, and worship the things of this world instead of the One who created it, we are failing to make the most of the opportunities that we have been given to find and live out our calling.

We usually think of time as a linear chronology—a succession of minutes, hours, days, and years. The word "chronology" comes directly from the Greek word *chronos*. However, the Greek language also has the word *kairos*, which is frequently translated in the Bible as "time," but in a different sense. While *chronos* is concerned with things happening in a certain order for a certain duration, *kairos* is about things happening at the proper time under the right circumstances.

God entrusts us with 1,440 minutes each day—minutes that are *chronos*, but can also be *kairos*. The essence of finding our calling comes from looking for the opportunities to use our money and our time directly for the purpose to which we have been called, instead of for pursuing our own desires. When we focus on short-term gratification, we receive the short-term reward of being happy for a few minutes or maybe a few hours. However, when we come to the end of our 1,440 minutes, our happiness is frequently replaced with the disillusionment of realizing there were things we should have done, but didn't—that we've wasted another day.

No one can go back and make a brand-new start, my friend; but anyone can start from here and make a brand-new end.
—Dan Zadra

This is perhaps one of the greatest comforts of life. No matter how many regrets we have in our past, each day is an opportunity to start again. All it takes is a little focus, a little discipline, and a clear sense of motivation.

Instead of wasting money, we can look for opportunities to invest it, not just in the markets, but also in people and causes that we care about.

By recognizing the ways in which we waste time, we can devise time management techniques and remove distractions from our environments to make our work time more effective and focused.

By becoming aware of the occasions when we devote our attentions and resources to less worthy endeavors, we can learn not only to place our worship where it belongs, but in doing so, set an example for our families to follow.

Perhaps one of the most freeing things that we can do is to acknowledge our role as stewards, rather than owners, of our material possessions. Let me say that again. *We are the stewards, not the owners, of our material possessions.* It is so important to understand that we don't "own" anything.

When we start to see our resources as tools rather than toys, as items to use in living out our calling rather than to simply consume for our own enjoyment, then the bigger picture becomes clearer. It takes a perspective shift of this nature to get us out of our mental ruts and self-serving habits. But sometimes these old habits die hard.

One of the things that a lot of people need to be careful of when considering their calling is that we tend to paint "Norman Rockwell pictures" in our mind.

One night on a couples' vacation to Texas, we were sitting around a campfire under the stars when one of the women dropped her defenses and opened up about how she was struggling to accept her son's decision to become a missionary. He was about to get married and go halfway around the world to live in China. She had grown up in a home where the family stayed close and shared meals together. She had a picture in her mind of how she wanted her life to be: She was the loving grandmother that all the grandkids would come to visit, just as she had visited her own grandmother.

Like one of those Rockwell illustrations, it was warm, safe and comforting.

I listened, then asked if I could share something for her to think about. She agreed.

I told her I thought she had painted a beautiful picture in her mind. "But maybe God has another painting," I said. "One that's very different. If you just allow God to paint His picture, you might find out that it's a much prettier painting."

I urged her to let that Norman Rockwell picture go. "Your son obviously feels like he has a calling to China to help and preach the Word. And in God's big picture, that's part of his masterpiece. You're going to have an eternity to spend with your son and your grandkids. Maybe it's more important that your grandchildren see their dad in his role as a missionary."

She thought about it, looked at me and said, "You are right. I have to let God paint the picture."

Now, many years later, the picture that God painted for her family is beautiful, very different and much better than anyone could have dreamed.

You see, I learned many years ago to let God paint my picture, and He is still painting. I could never have dreamed of being in a position where I would sit with CEOs of Fortune 100 companies, or be in a position to lead companies that seek a triple bottom line of economic, social and spiritual impact. I never dreamed I could be so blessed to have such a loving, caring family that is generous to the core.

You are in God's masterpiece

Many of us think we have a particular path we should follow, but it's the picture that *we* want, not the one God desires to paint. We're settling for a stick-figure crayon drawing when God offers us a beautiful masterpiece—if only we'd let go of the brush and let Him do the painting.

A lot of us are always thinking about and planning for the future. But when God was leading the children of Israel, He taught them a lesson: Live in the moment. Go out and get your daily manna, but don't get extra.

Yet what did the children of Israel do? They wanted to be in control, to hoard what they had in preparation for the unknowns of tomorrow. They didn't see the picture God was painting. And they suffered for it. We all suffer when, instead of looking for our calling, we let the world influence what we think our calling should be. The bottom line is that we can't fulfill God's plan for our lives if we are focused on our own plans.

> *Place your trust in the Eternal; rely on Him completely;*
> *never depend upon your own ideas and inventions.*
> *Give Him the credit for everything you accomplish,*
> *and He will smooth out and straighten the road that lies ahead.*[26]

Everyone on this planet has a purpose for his or her life. Finding that purpose is easier said than done. It usually doesn't happen by chance. Most people find their calling by the process of elimination—in other words, by wasting their time doing things that aren't "it." If what you are doing is sucking the life out of you and the thought of doing it fills you with dread, then that is not your calling. It isn't ever going to become your calling no matter how long you persist at it or how much of a tolerance you build up to the empty feeling that you get from it.

Many people lead lives that seem productive on the outside, but inside they are wasting away because they lack a sense of purpose. You can be a responsible citizen, working steadily at a respectable job, but if you don't feel that sense of purpose, then your life will just feel like you're on an endless merry-go-round.

Each of us has been chosen and called by God to do something specific with our time here on Earth. Even Jesus had a calling, and He was aware of it at an early age.

Luke's Gospel records the story of Mary and Joseph taking Jesus to Jerusalem for the Passover Feast when He was 12 years old. This was something they did every year with a large group of family and friends, so when the time came to go back home, they just went, not realizing that Jesus had stayed behind in Jerusalem.

After they'd started back, they traveled for a full day before they realized that Jesus wasn't with them. So Mary and Joseph went back to Jerusalem and frantically searched for Him all over the city. Finally, after three days, they went back to the temple—and there was Jesus speaking knowledgeably to the teachers. Mary, being a mom, had a high-speed "come-apart" and started tearing into Jesus right there in the temple courtyard about how worried she and Joseph were and how they were looking for Him everywhere.

Jesus responded:

> *"Why did you have to look for me? You should have known that I must be where my Father's work is."*[27]

Not only was Jesus thoroughly aware of His calling, He seemed surprised that His parents didn't get it. They were intensely focused on their present problem: finding their son. But Jesus, even at the age of 12, had the attitude of, "Where else would I be? This is my thing!"

> *Therefore, my brothers and sisters, make every effort to confirm your calling and election. For if you do these things, you will never stumble, and you will receive a rich welcome into the eternal kingdom of our Lord and Savior Jesus Christ.*[28]

This is the essence of what a calling is. What is it that makes you feel good about yourself? What is it that you like doing so much that you don't care whether you are paid to do it or not? What do you do that makes you say to yourself, "Yeah, this is how it should be?" When you start finding the answers to these questions, you begin to figure out what your calling is.

Your calling is the work that God uniquely designed you to do during your time on this earth.

Being God, His will and His work will always be done, with or without your cooperation. Sooner or later, we all find out that "with" yields a much more harmonious outcome in our lives. Maybe you have found that out for yourself when you finally gave in and did something you had been resisting for the longest time, like I did when I took the mission trip to Kenya. It's amazing what can happen when you give up the struggle and start thinking about God's plans more than your own. Then things just sort of fall into place, and you wonder, "Why didn't I do this sooner?"

The way to live a life where you stop asking yourself that question is to become more intentionally aware of your calling.

Since it is universal that we are NOT here primarily to build personal legacies, pursue our own happiness, or pile up toys, it makes sense that the common threads for our individual callings are:

- Bearing fruit that lasts beyond our lifetime without being concerned about whether or not our name is remembered in association with that legacy.
- Devoting our lives to the happiness and well-being of others.
- Sharing our blessings with those in need, wherever we may find them.

In other words, we are all called to CARE.

> What is the use of living, if it be not to strive for noble causes and to make this muddled world a better place for those who will live in it after we are gone? How else can we put ourselves in harmonious relation with the great verities and consolations of the infinite and the eternal? [29]

Anyone can choose a job or a career, but a calling is something that God has already chosen for you. As Ephesians 2:10 says, "It is God himself who has made us what we are and given us new lives from Christ Jesus; and long ages ago he planned that we should spend these lives in helping others."[30]

Who are you serving?

He wired you with a unique set of passions, gifts, and natural talents so that you could accomplish His purposes. Trying to live fulfilling lives by pleasing ourselves is a recipe for disaster. Trying to do that by pleasing other people is even worse. Nothing takes a person's eye off the ball quite like trying to please everyone all the time.

Serving people is not the same as pleasing people. How can you tell which one you're doing? If you are trying to please people, you will quickly become exhausted. On the other hand, if you are pleasing God by serving people, you will feel just as blessed as the people whom you are serving.

Focus instead on meeting needs rather than on trying to make people think you're a good person. Remember, it is God whom we are supposed to be glorifying, or shining the spotlight on, not ourselves. The best way we can do this is to fulfill our purpose by responding with swift obedience to His prompting in our lives.

Sometimes, this can mean stepping out in faith even when we're not entirely sure what we're doing or what the result will be.

It is important to understand that our "calling" doesn't necessarily mean our career. It can, but it doesn't have to. Maybe the person who always cooks the best dish at potlucks is called to be a professional chef—or maybe they are called to brighten the day of co-workers with a delicious dish. Maybe a person with artistic talent is called to be an artist for a living—or maybe they are called simply to create art for art's sake. Some people are called to full-time ministry and others simply to volunteer at church. Some people who are told they "missed their calling" really haven't. For these people, doing what they love for a living could turn their passion into drudgery.

For some people, their calling is as a volunteer. For others, their job is the area where they are called to make a difference. Expertise acquired from observation and experience can be applied to other areas of life: Some people learn a skill for their job that they end up being called to do as a volunteer in a different context. It doesn't always have to be spiritual. But it can be that way. Sometimes it's the day-to-day things like mowing the yard of an elderly neighbor or making a meal for a single parent. Maybe it's just a note saying, "Hey, thinking about you. Praying for you."

Maybe it's mentoring people, teaching them as they go on their journey in life. Maybe it's walking beside somebody who is in a low spot in life, and trying to help him or her pull back out of it. Maybe you have a calling that lasts a lifetime, or maybe you're called to different places during different seasons of your life.

It only takes a moment to be kind,
but the results can last a lifetime.

I love to wash my car, because when I'm done I can see that I've accomplished something. As human beings, we tend to be results-driven. This can make it difficult for us in those times when we don't get to see the results of our efforts right away. We love to plant the seeds, but sometimes we can get frustrated when we find out that we don't get to be the one who reaps the harvest.

I think we'll get to see that in heaven. Somebody asked me once, "Do you know what the most often-spoken word in heaven is going to be?" I said I didn't, and he said, "AHH!" That's where it will all come together, and we will see how our little bit of help in a single circumstance really affected generations to come. What a joy it will be to see all the connections!

For now, we can only see a dim and blurry picture of things,
as when we stare into polished metal. I realize that everything
I know is only part of the big picture. But one day, when
Jesus arrives, we will see clearly, face-to-face. In that day,
I will fully know just as I have been wholly known by God.[31]

Sometimes your calling is not simple to find, but sometimes it hits you like a hockey puck. "Oh! So *this* is what I'm supposed to do!" I know for me in my own journey it took a few years.

In 1988, I got a phone call from Ward Correll, one of my directors. I was 28 years old and had just been named CEO of a bank. It was at the end of the year and he asked me, "James, what is your most important job next year?"

I could have given him an answer like, "Get X percent return on equity. Get past-dues below X amount of dollars. Get interest margins up X percent." I could have given him all kinds of metrics that could have been measured. Looking back, I can hardly believe I did it, but I asked the director, "What do *you* think my most important job is next year?"

I responded to his question with a question. As it turned out, I asked the right question. He told me to grow people. He said, "If you grow people, they will grow your business. If you grow people, they will grow you. You must grow so they can grow. Grow people."

And he hung up the phone.

I reflected on that advice and wisdom, but it really wasn't until about four years later that I discovered it was the platform God had given me. I remind myself of this calling by carrying a personal mission statement with me wherever I go.

MISSION STATEMENT

**To use the platform that God has given me,
To GROW PEOPLE, both known and unknown,
rich and poor, regardless of race. Growth Spiritually, Growth
Emotionally, Growth Professionally.**

I plan to accomplish this by providing:

H—Hope is the greatest medicine in the world.

E—Encouragement, because we all grow our best when we are respected and appreciated.

L—Love, not as the world knows, but Christlike.

P—Pleasure will be mine from knowing that I have fulfilled God's plan and have made a difference in the lives of others.

So that's my purpose; that's my calling. But while you can write a nice mission statement, that alone doesn't help you live your calling. You have to do it.

Don't, I beg you, only hear the message, but put it into practice; otherwise, you are merely deluding yourselves. The man who simply hears and does nothing about it is like a man catching the reflection of his own face in a mirror. He sees himself, it is true, but he goes on with whatever he was doing without the slightest recollection of what sort of person he saw in the mirror.[32]

Ever since I heard one of our wise directors talk about erosion, I often ask myself: "What am I doing to stop the erosion from generation to generation in my life and in my family?"

About a year ago, I started sending my grandson a Bible verse about every two weeks. I ask him to memorize that Bible verse, and then call and tell me what it says and what it means.

We have also tried to teach our children the joy of generosity. One year at Thanksgiving we gave each of our children money, and told them that what we wanted for Christmas was for them to give the money away and then tell us at Christmas how they did it. They could do anything they wanted with it.

Another year, we combined their money and told them we would give the money wherever they wanted. They could give it all to one place or they could give it to several places, but they had to talk with each other and all agree about the allocation.

This year, we told our children that we would match any donations they made, dollar for dollar, up to five hundred dollars each. Or if they went and worked at a ministry or a mission, we would give up to twenty dollars an hour to donate. My son in New York gets up every Saturday morning and volunteers for Meals on Wheels. To be more accurate, it's really "Meals on Heels," because in New York, it makes more sense to do it on foot. If he spends three hours a week doing that, I give sixty dollars to the ministry of his choice.

My family and friends aren't the only thing I think about, though. I also wonder what I can do to stop the erosion in my business life. How does the leadership team in our companies, that has been built through the vision of Jess Correll, turn it over to the next generation and make sure they understand that their purpose is always to serve God's Kingdom? I have found that the same principles we employ at home can bear fruit in the workplace as well.

Recently, our company gave every employee a hundred dollars, because we wanted our people to give back to the community, to understand generosity. I have heard some amazing stories of how employees gave that money to someone in need. What is especially impressive is that several of them said, "Before I did this, I would have never seen that person."

One employee walked over to a homeless man near a dumpster at a car wash. With his wife and preschool-age son watching from the car, he talked to the guy for a few minutes and gave him a twenty-dollar bill. When he got back to the car, his wife was tearing up, their son was asking questions and, as they pulled out, the homeless man waved goodbye to them. That night, his son included the homeless man in his prayers. That young man and his wife have decided that now they're going to keep money in their wallets so that when they see somebody in need, they can help.

That's growing people. That's growing that couple; it's growing that child. And hopefully they'll understand that and know that they're doing something good. We make a living by what we get, but we make a life by what we give.

Form a plan, and follow through

Don't feel bad if you can't instantly figure out what your calling is. You're not alone.

Here are a few practical exercises to help get you started on your journey.

1. Make a list of everything that you enjoy and can do with relative ease.

These can be small or large things. Write down everything you can think of. When you are finished, take a break for a few minutes and then come back to your list. Look at each item on your list and ask yourself which of those things put your happiness above the needs of others. Cross those things off. Those are the things that will get in the way of you finding your calling.

2. Make a material possessions inventory.

First, make a list of the material things that you already own. Next, make a list of the things you don't have, but that you would like to have. Finally, take your best guess at the cost of each item on these lists.

Then, take a critical look at each item on those lists. What are the things that you could honestly live without? Draw an X next to those items, and then add up the total value of the items you marked with an X. You might be surprised at the total.

As we learn to be content by trusting God to meet our needs, we find ourselves focusing more on the needs of others. These first two exercises can help us clarify what drives us and what resources we either have available now or may have in the future to use as a tool in living out our calling.

3. Pray and listen.

Now you have a list of things that you are gifted at, a guide to be more unselfish, and you have an idea of how much money you can free up in your budget going forward to help make some of these things happen. Now comes the scary part.

Ask God what He wants you to do from your list. Then wait for the answer. The answer could come from any of several sources. Canadian pastor Henry Blackaby explains, "God speaks by the Holy Spirit through the Bible, prayer, circumstances, and the church to reveal Himself, His purposes, and His ways."[33]

Sometimes the answer is directly in the Bible.

Sometimes we have a thought that we know we didn't come up with on our own, and we share that thought with another believer, who "gets a witness" in his or her heart that the message is an answer to prayer.

Sometimes we encounter a series of events that is just too perfectly arranged to be a coincidence.

Be open to all these possibilities.

Understand that the answer may not come right away. You may have to ask more than once. You may get an answer that wasn't even on your list. The important thing is to expect that your prayer will be answered in its due time.

If you want to know what God wants you to do, ask him, and he will gladly tell you, for he is always ready to give a bountiful supply of wisdom to all who ask him; he will not resent it. But when you ask him, be sure that you really expect him to tell you, for a doubtful mind will be as unsettled as a wave of the sea that is driven and tossed by the wind; and every decision you then make will be uncertain, as you turn first this way and then that. If you don't ask with faith, don't expect the Lord to give you any solid answer.[34]

As you develop these disciplines of prayer and looking outside yourself, you may notice that other things in your life begin to change. You may find your perspective and priorities shifting from immediate gratification to eternal significance. You might find yourself cutting activities out of your schedule that conflict with your newfound priorities. You may become more aware of how you are spending your time and your money. You may start seeing people differently, or even noticing people that you had never noticed before. Most importantly, you will find your trust and reliance on God growing.

CARE

ATTITUDE

The shelves of bookstores are filled with books about attitude. Attitude is *everything*.

The Attitude of Gratitude. Attitude 101. Think Positive. The consensus seems to be that having the right attitude makes all the difference in life. When it comes to living out your calling, this is definitely true. Just as it is true that you can't go somewhere you've never been by doing what you've always done, it also makes sense that you can't do what you've never done by having the same attitude that you've always had.

The purpose of this chapter is not so much to direct you to what choices you should make, but to help you understand the motivations behind the choices you are already making. Remember, it's not all about knowing the right answer, but also asking the right question. The questions you will want to ask yourself throughout this chapter are, "How is my current attitude?" and after that, "What changes do I need to make concerning my attitude?"

Everyone you meet brings joy to your life—some when they enter, some when they leave.

How do you want to be remembered? Most of us, especially when we are younger, feel driven to leave our mark on the world.

Think about some of the people who have made the greatest impact on your life, the ones who have been the most influential in shaping you into the person you are today. You might recall a teacher who opened you up to a whole new way of thinking, or a coach who taught you about teamwork. Maybe you think about a pastor who challenged you to grow spiritually, a mentor who helped you address your failings by being transparent about his or her own, or the person who first invited you into a group when you were a stranger. Whoever these people are in your life, what was it that they said or did that stayed with you years, or even decades, later?

Most likely, it was their qualities and attributes that you found attractive. Their authenticity, humility, selflessness, encouragement, integrity, gentleness, caring, inspiration, enlightenment and unconditional love—these are the reasons why you still have fond memories of them today. What do they all have in common? The people who had the greatest positive impact on us likely had great attitudes.

One person (among many) who had a big impact on my life was my grandfather. His name was Una Bandy and I called him "Papaw."

Papaw worked at Royal Crown Cola for many years, starting work at 5:30 every morning, working until 4:00 every afternoon. He did that six days a week. On Sundays he drove the church bus, never missing a Sunday for over twenty years. He picked up elderly ladies in the community and then went to the Kentucky School for the Deaf to pick up the children.

He always had a smile. I never heard him complain. I know he loved the Lord and loved his family. He was a man who never made much in the way of income, but he felt rich because he understood that happiness is not having what you want, it's wanting what you have.

I was privileged to ride the bus to church with him on many Sundays. When I was a teenager, we worked together on my dad's farm, mowing, fixing fences and feeding cattle. Believe me, as a teenager I hated hearing his pickup pull in the driveway at 7 a.m.

to head to the farm for a day's work. But I now know the lessons I was learning were worth gold, as he instilled in me the value of providing an honest day's work. I can see him in my mind right now, reading his *Open Windows* devotional, with his worn-out Bible open to the scripture. At the end of his reading, he would remove his glasses and pray. What he taught me was important to the Lord, it was important to my Papaw Bandy and it is now very important to me.

I have so much respect for him. If you pull into my garage you will see my collection of Royal Crown Cola thermometers, various RC collectables, his RC work shirt with his name on the left near the coffee stain that he seemed to leave on every shirt. It makes me smile just to think of him.

What did I learn?

- To be content with what you have.
- Hard work never hurt you.
- Dedication.
- Focus.
- Whatever you do, do your best.
- Love others more than yourself.

Do you see what this means—all these pioneers who blazed the way, all these veterans cheering us on? It means we'd better get on with it.[35]

Pawpaw Bandy's attitude changed my life. In my imagination, he is still cheering me on when things get tough.

So ask yourself: As you reflect on those attributes and attitudes of the people who played such a role for you, how many of the same attributes have you displayed in your own life?

Remember that just as these people had an impact on you, so you are also having an impact on the people with whom you come into contact every day.

You may not even realize how many people are watching you, but rest assured that they are. This is especially true if you have children. Parents are the most influential teachers in a child's life.

How aware are you of the image that you are projecting to your children?

Attitude is so much more than just image, though. Anyone can intentionally project an image that represents how he or she would like to be viewed by the world, but your attitude reflects who you REALLY are. What is in your heart will find a way through the cracks in every mask that we wear for the public. People notice this hypocrisy. Maybe not everyone, but some do. The word "hypocrite" comes directly from the term used in the ancient Greek theater, meaning "an actor who hides behind a mask and pretends to be somebody else." Have you ever caught yourself doing that? It's never a good situation when your mouth says one thing to the world but your attitude says something completely different.

Let your light shine

David Kinnaman is the president of the Barna Group, a research organization that studies the dynamics of faith and culture. In his first book, *UnChristian: What a New Generation Really Thinks About Christianity... And Why It Matters*, Kinnaman makes several observations regarding the hypocritical image that American Christians have acquired, the chief one being that their lives don't match their beliefs. Kinnaman writes, "In virtually every study we conduct, representing thousands of interviews every year, born-again Christians fail to display much attitudinal or behavioral evidence of transformed lives." To back up this statement, Kinnaman points out that his research found that while 84 percent of young people outside the church said they knew a Christian personally, only 15 percent of the same group thought that the lifestyles of the Christians they knew varied significantly from that of non-Christians.[36]

A key area in which one might suppose that Christians would stand out from non-Christians is in the practice of giving. Unfortunately, the evidence appears to suggest otherwise. Since 1991, John and Sylvia Ronsvalle have provided an annual report called *The State of Church Giving*. Their findings show that while the average American's income has increased by 131 percent in inflation-adjusted dollars between 1968 and 2011, the percentage that Christians donate has declined. In some denominations, giving has declined by more than 50 percent since the first report.[37]

This decline in giving can be directly tied to an erosion of attitude. In his book, *Growing True Disciples*, George Barna laments the fact that, in their attitudes and actions, Christians appear little different from nonbelievers.[38] So if our attitudes reflect who we really are underneath our masks, then the actions springing from our attitudes allow other people to see what's in our hearts, whether or not we intended to remove our masks.

You are like light for the whole world. A city built on top of
a hill cannot be hidden, and no one would light a lamp
and put it under a clay pot. A lamp is placed on a lampstand,
where it can give light to everyone in the house.
Make your light shine, so that others will see the good
that you do and will praise your Father in heaven.[39]

Just as you cannot throw a rock into the middle of a still pond without making a splash, so you cannot be in the world without your attitude having an impact on the people around you. The ripples emanating from the rock you throw into the pond eventually reach all the way to the edge—but have you noticed that it is not just one ripple, but many? The concentric circles of ripples on a pond are a good illustration of how your attitude can have far-reaching implications in society.

Since attitude leads directly to behavior, and behavior is what others see on the outside, whoever observes your behavior directly is in the "splash zone." Whatever attitude your behavior displays is going to have an immediate effect on those nearest to you. If you have a grateful attitude and are at peace, you will show this by the smile on your face, or by making friendly eye contact with people you meet. Perhaps, if some of those people are having a bad day, encountering your positive attitude will lift their spirits and change their outlook. And as these people encounter other people throughout their day, the splash you made with your positive attitude will ripple outward through those people, and the ones they meet, and so on. You might never see it, but with every person you meet, there is a potential for another person several ripples away to have a life-changing experience as an indirect result of whatever type of "attitude rock" you threw to make that splash. So the question is, what type of rocks are you throwing?

Things don't go wrong and break your heart so you can
become bitter and give up. They happen to break you down
and build you up so you can be all that you were intended to be.[40]

Everybody has trials and tribulations at various points in life. While we don't have the luxury of choosing our circumstances, we do get to choose how we respond to them. It is the attitude we have chosen to cultivate that will determine what those responses will be.

When I met my wife, we were both divorced. She had been single for several years when we met. Eventually, when we started discussing having a life together, one of the things that she mentioned to me was that she never wanted to forget how hard it was to be single. At the time, I figured that if she remembered how miserable she had been when she was single, then she would always be happy to be married to me! What she actually was saying was a bit different.

She really meant that she had a heart for single women and moms, having been one herself, and having gone through what they go through on a daily basis. After we were married, with the blessing of the leadership of our church, she started a single moms' ministry. It started with just a few ladies. It grew to many. Through this ministry, my wife and others are able to encourage single moms by helping with school supplies at the beginning of a new year or providing daycare around Christmas. When moms are struggling financially, they provide money for car repairs and groceries. She just really loved on these single moms.

Of course, this ministry didn't come without challenges. For example, one goal was to help advise these single moms if they started into new relationships. However, some of the other volunteers twisted that goal and tried to turn it into a couples' ministry, trying to actively fix these women up with men, rather than focusing on meeting the women where they were.

Nevertheless, the ministry has survived the challenges and still continues today, even though we have moved to another state. Lives are still being changed to this day, all because my wife had the attitude that she was going to take something traumatic in her life and turn it into something good for others.

Many people are in a rut and a rut is nothing but a grave—
with both ends kicked out.[41]

Sometimes we have periods in our lives when we just find ourselves stuck in a rut. I had a difficult time in my life where I found myself in a deep one. One day as I was feeling sorry for myself, my good friend Jess Correll looked at me and said, "You know, I'm sick of looking at you.

"You've got a choice here. You're either going to let this point in time in your life tear you completely apart, or you're going to grow from it and be better from it."

I had two thoughts go through my mind in a split second. The first was, "Who does he think he is?" And the second was, "He's right." So from that day on I have tried to have the attitude that everything that happens to us in life will make us either bitter or better. It's up to us to choose which way our attitude is going to go, but it is useful to find a mentor to help us make the right choices. We can all benefit from a friend who will tell us what we NEED to hear about our attitude rather than to tickle our ears and try to make us feel good about ourselves where we are when there's something that needs changing. I have been fortunate enough since then to have opportunities to assume that role in other people's lives and pass this lesson along.

One time I had spoken to a young woman who had been doing something that she shouldn't have been doing. And she felt judged; she felt like everybody was down on her. I walked in one time and told her to quit looking down at her shoes. I said, "Get your head up. You made a mistake. You repented. If other people want to judge you, that's their problem. I know you; you won't do the same thing again. You will go forth from here and do well, and use this experience to make yourself better, not bitter." And she did.

The remarkable thing we have is a choice every day regarding the attitude we will embrace for that day. We cannot change our past... We cannot change the fact that people will act in a certain way. We cannot change the inevitable. The only thing we can do is play on the one string we have, and that is our attitude.[42]

In the previous chapter, you began the process of discerning your calling by asking yourself the question, "What do I CARE about?" Now, as we discuss attitude, the question is, "How do your choices reflect that you CARE?" To understand how to answer that question, however, we need to examine the motivations, or attitudes, behind the choices that we make, since our attitude is what drives our actions.

Things which matter most must never be at the
mercy of things which matter least.
—Johann Wolfgang von Goethe[43]

What matters most to you? Whatever that is, it will fall into one of
three basic categories: the things you have, the things you do, and
the people with whom you interact.

Usually, the first things that come to mind when we think about
the things we have are our material possessions—the things we
can hold or look at. This also includes money, both in and of
itself and as a vehicle to obtain more possessions. The key to
understanding your attitude toward money is in that word, "possessions." This word indicates ownership. So the question that
you need to answer for yourself is, "Whose money or stuff is this,
really?"

An attitude that many of us have regarding our possessions and
our wealth is that it is ours because we worked for it. Our possessions, and the lifestyle that they represent, are a reward for
our efforts. If this were the case, then our primary motivation for
working would be to get the paycheck to fund that lifestyle. If this
lifestyle is what matters most to us, then we will have received our
reward in full.

The LORD owns the earth and all it contains,
the world and all who live in it.[44]

Go back to those lists you made in Chapter 2, the ones with the
things that made you happy and the things you could live without.
These were a ballpark measurement of your attitudes toward your
treasure, specifically, to what extent you felt you needed material
possessions to determine your level of fulfillment. They were also
an introduction to reflecting on an attitude of contentment, or
separating your wants from your actual needs. People with an attitude of entitlement will guard money and possessions and keep as
much as they can for themselves. On the other hand, people who
have the attitude that nothing really belongs to them will cultivate
the habit of stewardship—taking care of something that is not
theirs. Good stewards have a deeper sense of trust that their own
needs will be met, which frees up their minds to focus more on the
needs of others. They see themselves as managers, not owners.

The starfish story

Many of us in this country have a great deal more than we need. Therefore, if your goal is to develop the attitude of focusing on the needs of others, a question you might ask yourself is, "How much money do I have that I would not miss?" Answering this question requires a good deal of reflection as well as hands-on budgeting. However, when you have an accurate picture of how much money you have spent on unnecessary pursuits, then you will know exactly how much you have to work with as you start to develop a plan of action for your calling. As you start to see the actual possibilities of the impact you are capable of having with your treasure, see if your attitude doesn't shift from, "I can't make a difference," to, "I can make THIS MUCH of a difference." After you have had some time to put this attitude into action, you might even find yourself thinking about how you will manage money you haven't even made yet. The size of your impact on the world is only limited by the size of the vision that your attitude allows.

> *While wandering a deserted beach at dawn, stagnant in my work, I saw a man in the distance bending and throwing as he walked the endless stretch toward me. As he came near, I could see that he was throwing starfish, abandoned on the sand by the tide, back into the sea. When he was close enough I asked him why he was working so hard at this strange task. He said that the sun would dry the starfish and they would die. I said to him that I thought he was foolish. There were thousands of starfish on miles and miles of beach. One man alone could never make a difference. He smiled as he picked up the next starfish. Hurling it far into the sea he said, "It makes a difference for this one." I abandoned my writing and spent the morning throwing starfish."*[45]

In Chapter 2, we discovered the very humbling statistic that the average person wastes four out of every ten minutes of consciousness immersed in visual media. And yet, if we are honest with ourselves, doesn't it always feel like we never have time to complete the tasks that we feel we ought to be completing?

Since we all have the same amount of time, we all have the same amount of potential availability. Many of us put quite a bit of effort into trying to manage our available time in order to maximize our sense of productivity. Some do this by prioritizing their schedule in order to get the most important things done first. This shows a task-oriented attitude. Others view time management with more of a values-centered attitude. Instead of prioritizing their schedules, these people focus on scheduling their priorities. The goal is still to take care of the most important things first; however, instead of focusing on the tasks themselves, this technique is more focused on the impact that the completion of the tasks will have.

Although these two approaches differ slightly, what they have in common is that they both primarily concern the productivity of the individual who is making the to-do list. An entirely different approach would be to have a people-centered attitude toward the events of your day. While there's nothing wrong with having a plan of action for your day, cultivating an attitude of availability trains you to keep your eyes open for people who have a need that you are able to meet. Where a task-centered attitude might prompt a response of, "Yes, that is a worthy cause, but I'm not sure I can fit it into my schedule," a people-centered attitude prods us into immediate action when we see a need. Because our attitude is more focused on the world around us, we are able to respond to those we encounter rather than wasting time trying to determine where these people and their situations ought to fit into our hierarchy of priorities. After all, it's impossible to bemoan the time you don't have to do something if you're already busy doing it.

Every human activity, except sin, can be done for God's pleasure if you do it with an attitude of praise. You can wash dishes, repair a machine, sell a product, write a computer program, grow a crop, and raise a family for the glory of God.[46]

What is it that you are really good at doing? Not just in the sense of a career or job duties, but also in everyday life? Living your calling effectively involves your best attitude meeting your greatest aptitude. Skills can be learned, of course, and growth in new areas can certainly be part of a calling. However, it makes sense that we should be the most efficient where we are the most proficient.
We all have times in our lives when we are tempted to not give our best, don't we?

Sometimes when we're tired, or if there's something else we'd rather be doing, it is all too easy to just say, "Good enough," and cut a corner or two on the job we're doing. Of course, when we do this, we are thinking about ourselves and about our own comfort. But think about a time when you have been on the receiving end of this kind of service. Have you ever gone out to eat at a restaurant to find your table not thoroughly wiped off and a couple of French fries under your seat? Then you get to the bottom of your glass and have to wait awhile to get a refill? And your server never makes eye contact and doesn't ask you if there's anything else that they can get for you?

You're probably not going to leave a very good tip, right? Yet, the folks at that restaurant on that day did not make it their goal to give you poor service. Even so, an example like this one makes it clear that "good enough" really isn't good enough.

And don't just do the minimum that will get you by. Do your best. Work from the heart for your real Master, for God, confident that you'll get paid in full when you come into your inheritance. Keep in mind always that the ultimate Master you're serving is Christ. The sullen servant who does shoddy work will be held responsible. Being a follower of Jesus doesn't cover up bad work.[47]

So what is the best antidote to the phenomenon of drifting into a "good enough" mentality? It is the difference between having an attitude of meeting expectations and exceeding expectations. Think about restaurants again. Who do you give good tips to? The servers who go out of their way to make your dining experience special. They don't just bring you your food, fill up your drink, bring you the check and go away. These people introduce themselves by name, tell you the specials before you ask, know all the sides and salad dressings without having to look them up, make sure your glass never hits bottom, and go out of their way to make sure that you have everything you need. In short, these are the people who have decided in advance that they are going to deliver MORE than expected.

When you have this kind of an attitude, you WILL be noticed. Some people who notice you will be inspired by your example and want to follow it or join you in your work. However, others will not. They might say that you are making them look bad by going the extra mile when they're settling for "good enough."

Have you ever experienced this in your own workplace? It is easy to spot the folks who are just there for a paycheck. They are neither inspired nor inspiring. Of course, there's nothing wrong with earning a paycheck—we all need to support ourselves and our families. But you can always tell when employees really see what their calling is. They aren't using their profession as just a means of earning money. What they're concerned with is making sure that they're providing something extra. These are the people that you're drawn to at work, the ones who see the big picture.

But this sort of attitude isn't just for the workplace. It's a lifestyle that you carry with you wherever you go and whatever you do. Everything from mission work in a Third World country to interacting with neighbors to raising your kids has eternal implications. While another human may sign our paychecks, our true reward comes in heaven, and as we have given, so we shall receive. This is why it is so important to serve with a cheerful heart and to use our talents with the attitude that nothing but our best will do. When we do our best, the quality of our work will naturally improve.

It isn't just our attitude that makes ripples, but also the PRODUCT of our attitude. When you are throwing a rock into a pond, where you throw the rock affects the size and breadth of the ripples. Getting it to kerplunk in just the right space somewhere in the middle can make the water ripple outward all the way to each bank. In the same way, expending your treasure, time, and talents strategically will give you the greatest impact.

Take a few moments and think about the places you go on an average day. Some places are going to be the same from day to day, as are some of the people you see. Over time, these places and faces become as familiar to you as old furniture; however, when you begin each day with the attitude of intentionally looking for people and situations in which to use your resources, you will see these people in a different light.

Indeed this is part of your calling. For Christ suffered for you and left you a personal example, and wants you to follow in his steps. "Who committed no sin, nor was guile found in his mouth." Yet when he was insulted he offered no insult in return. When he suffered he made no threats of revenge. He simply committed his cause to the one who judges fairly.[48]

Jesus knew what His purpose was. He knew He came to die for our sins, but He also knew that He had other things to do before He died. He had to spend forty days in the wilderness, then confront Satan. He had to heal the sick, give sight to the blind, teach the disciples. And, of course, He had to suffer leading up to His crucifixion. He did all of this because He was single-mindedly motivated by the attitude of giving Himself completely to the relationship with humanity that He came down from Heaven to forge.

Never act from motives of rivalry or personal vanity, but in humility think more of each other than you do of yourselves. None of you should think only of his own affairs, but should learn to see things from other people's point of view.

Let Christ himself be your example as to what your attitude should be.

For he, who had always been God by nature, did not cling to his prerogatives as God's equal, but stripped himself of all privilege by consenting to be a slave by nature and being born as mortal man. And, having become man, he humbled himself by living a life of utter obedience, even to the extent of dying, and the death he died was the death of a common criminal.[49]

Attitude is a choice. But sometimes we make choices without being aware that we are making them. This is especially true with attitude. If we are not making a conscious effort to monitor our attitudes, it becomes all too easy to let them drift where our moods take us.

'You're really grumpy'

A good way to prevent this is to learn to see yourself from the perspective of others by simply asking them if they have noticed any erosion in your attitude. This can sometimes be more challenging than it sounds, though.

Have you ever noticed that when you ask someone to give you honest criticism, it usually takes several attempts to get a straight answer? Imagine that you are a boss and you ask an employee for honest feedback. The employee would probably answer with, "I think you're doing a great job, and I like working here." Then you can ask the exact same question a second time, and you might get an answer like, "Well, the reason you are where you are is because of your experience and skills, and I respect that." It isn't until you ask them a third time that you really get to the heart of the matter. As an employer, I have done this many times with employees. One time I went through this ritual with a woman who worked for me. The third time I asked her how I was doing, she came right out and said, "Well, you can be really grumpy in the morning, and that's kind of a downer." The next day, she came into my office to apologize to me. I told her it wasn't necessary.

My grumpy attitude was carrying forward to people on my staff just because they worked around me. But by becoming aware of the situation, I was able to do something about it. And I have made sure from that day forward to check my attitude first thing in the morning. This has only been possible because I have learned to concern myself not just with the rocks, but also the ripples.

> *I never want to underestimate the example I am setting. My kids are watching how I live, and the choices I make have rippling effects down through the generations. I can choose to do nothing and let my children be swept up in the current of empty materialism that is rampant in our culture, or I can choose to live a different way by living generously.*[50]

It has been said that having an others-centered attitude will lead to a life of generosity.

While that may sometimes be true, it isn't the whole story. It is possible to give out of a sense of duty, obligation, or even guilt. In these instances, the act of giving might temporarily meet another's need; however, the attitude behind it is not likely to be contagious. For a lifestyle of generosity to be sustainable, actions must spring from a genuine interest in helping other people.

The quickest way to evaluate your own motivation is to form the habit of frequently asking yourself, "What do I CARE about?" Are you motivated by a desire to lift people up and spur them on, or do you want to be seen doing good in order to receive the praise of others? If the rocks you're throwing aren't producing the ripples that you had hoped for, then it might be time to carefully consider your motivations so that you can change whatever needs changing in your attitude.

> *You can give without loving, but you can never love without giving. The great acts of love are done by those who are habitually performing small acts of kindness. We pardon to the extent that we love. Love is knowing that even when you are alone, you will never be lonely again. And great happiness of life is the conviction that we are loved. Loved for ourselves. And even loved in spite of ourselves.*[51]

Back when I used to officiate basketball games, there was a certain young man who had a particularly good attitude. When he had a call go against him, he didn't argue. When that young man graduated, I was in a position to offer him a job at the bank. After he came to work, I watched him for a few days and I could see that he was behaving differently toward the loan officers than he was toward the tellers. I took that young man aside and told him: "Look at these tellers. They all know that you're being groomed to be a loan officer someday. They themselves will never take a loan application. They don't want to look at somebody and say, 'yes' or 'no' or negotiate on terms.

"But they see our customers every day and know things about them. They can help you... or not. In order for them to help you, you have to help them. And here's how you do it. You know those heavy bags of coins that they have to carry around? I watched you yesterday sitting around while a woman carried two of those bags of coins to the vault. Every morning when they come in to work, they have to get all this stuff out of the vault so that they can start the day's work, and it takes ten or fifteen minutes. Why not do that for them, so when they come in, they can get started earlier?" This young man's mom and dad had given him instruction about a wise man seeking counsel, but he didn't yet realize that counsel can come from somebody below or beside him as well as from above him.

Now fast-forward about twenty years. This man is now the CEO of a bank. He told me that he began to realize that everybody plays a role in helping someone else succeed, and that the servant's heart he cultivated as a young man was the key to his success.
From a worldly perspective, success is about climbing the corporate ladder. The problem is that a lot of times you've got the ladder up against the wrong wall, the wall of selfish ambition. Finding your calling, in essence, is finding the right wall to lean your ladder against. If you're climbing a ladder that's leaning on the right wall, your attitude will eventually improve as you climb it. This may not happen right away. Sometimes doing the right thing because it's the right thing can really be a chore, but in the end, you'll be able to look back on the fruits of your labor and be glad.

"Whenever you're in conflict with someone, there is one factor that can make the difference between damaging your relationship and deepening it. That factor is attitude."
—William James

Not all people have the same motivation for doing what they do. Some people want their life's work to have lasting meaning, but some just want the world to remember their names.

Some give cheerfully out of their abundance as an expression of gratitude for their material blessings while some give to draw attention to themselves and their great wealth. Some strive to be better; some choose to be bitter. Some want to relate rightly to others, and some just want to be right. Some rise above their difficult circumstances, and others stay in a constant state of emotional devastation because they find it easier to remain where they are than to step out in faith. Some people are in it for the money, while some focus their energies on making the world a better place, or giving glory to the God that they serve by always giving their best. Some are here to get, and some are here to give. Some are all about themselves, and some are all about others.

Not everyone you meet is going to take the same approach to life that you are. The more you work on developing your own caring attitude, the more aware you will become of people whose motivations might not be in line with yours. This sort of conflict can really rattle us if we let it. We might think that our efforts are in vain if we encounter someone whose motivation seems to be all wrong, yet they also have the appearance of being successful. Or the opposite could also be true. You may begin to be successful because of the change in your attitude, and then you might encounter someone who is openly resentful of your success. Since nobody really enjoys being told that they are "doing it wrong," how then should we respond when we find ourselves in conflict with someone who appears to have their motivations out of whack? The attitude we should have can be summed up in a single word: forgiveness.

"One forgives to the degree that one loves."
—Francois VI Duc de La Rochefoucauld

One of the worst attitudes that we can possibly have is an attitude of unforgiveness.

Holding a grudge is like drinking poison and expecting the person you're mad at to die. For this reason, it makes no sense to harbor a spirit of offense when you encounter somebody whom you feel has impure motivations. Remember, attitude is a choice. If you choose to have bad thoughts about somebody else, those thoughts will manifest in your words and actions.

Have you ever been around somebody who gossips and tears down other people behind their backs? You didn't really enjoy that person's company, did you?

So don't be that person.

You have power over your own attitude; therefore, the best thing you can do in a situation like that is to forgive the gossiper in your heart for their unseemly behavior. Then, if possible, try to set the best example you can for that other person with your own good attitude. Rather than tell others how they are wrong, just show them what "right" looks like. Of course, this approach will only work if you are behaving authentically. You can't fake a good attitude, not for long anyway. Anybody can paste a plastic smile onto their face, but if you're not truly motivated by a desire to put others first, to make the world a better place, to CARE, then it won't be long before people catch on to what you're up to. If you're gossiping in the break room, but smiling at your work station, anyone who has seen you in both places already knows which one is the real you.

So to help develop your attitude, practice authenticity. To feed and foster an attitude of putting others first, you first have to acknowledge deep down that you aren't really better than the people with bad attitudes you've encountered. Whenever you are around someone or hear about someone behaving in a way that offends you somehow, take a breath and think about the things you have done wrong in the past. When you do this, be careful not to backslide into feelings of guilt about your past. That's not what this is about. This exercise is all about shifting your perspective. When you develop this habit, you will find it easier to be more transparent publicly about your own fears and failures. What you will find is that people are more attracted to your attitude of authenticity than they would have been if you were playing the judge of their lives.

By showing others grace—by giving them room to grow—you will also grow. And by showing them respect, you will earn theirs as well.

CARE

RESPECT

*"Guys, you need to figure out in any relationship and
every relationship, why are you in it?
Are you in it to give or to get?"*
— Bob Warren

Every relationship that we have as human beings has two main
dynamics at work: what we are putting into the relationship, and
what we are getting out of it. If our primary motive is to give, then
our attitude will be, "What can I do for you?" If we are in a relationship to get, it will be more like, "What can you do for me?"

It isn't necessarily a bad thing to evaluate what someone else can
do for you. Just about anyone who has ever helped you was able
to do so because you recognized that being acquainted with that
person was going to be beneficial to you in some way. The difference is in the PRIMARY motivation. Are you there primarily to get
something, or do you want the relationship to be one of mutual
benefit? Are you there to get your back scratched, or are you doing
some scratching as well?

These dynamics exist in every relationship. Probably the most obvious example is marriage. Many people enter into a marital relationship with visions of a perfect fifty-fifty partnership where both spouses contribute equally, and life is in perfect balance.

Except it never works that way.

Instead, what tends to happen is this: At first, each spouse begins by focusing on what he or she perceives his or her own 50 percent to be. Sooner or later, though, a day comes when one spouse has a need that isn't met. Maybe dinner wasn't on the table one night when one of them came home from work, or someone's favorite coffee mug wasn't clean because the other one didn't do the dishes. Then the perspective shifts from, "I'm doing my part," to, "My spouse isn't doing their part." Without them realizing, the marriage is beginning to turn into a "What have you done for ME lately?" relationship, as each dwells on the ways the other isn't doing enough. If they aren't careful about communicating with each other, resentment will build, and that marriage will eventually be in serious trouble.

Marriage math is based on multiplication, not addition. So rather than 50 percent plus 50 percent equaling 100 percent, what ends up happening is that her 50 percent times his 50 percent equals 25 percent. This is unavoidable, because if you are focused on putting 50 percent into a relationship, then you are limiting your own contribution. As soon as you hit your half, you're done. If the relationship is going to continue, you must ALWAYS be "doing your part." Because the minute you stop, you will begin to worry about what your spouse ISN'T doing. And if that's what you're looking for, then that's what you'll find. The result is that both spouses putting in half the effort yields a failing marriage.

There's a better way to do marriage, of course. Instead of spouses keeping score about how much work is getting done or how many needs are being met (or not), they can instead choose to meet each other's needs first. When spouses are concerned about what they are putting in, they put more in. Then the math starts to look more like 100/100 than 50/50. And in marriage math, 100 percent times 100 percent equals 10,000 percent! Each person is not going to be able to give 100 percent effort 100 percent of the time, but when each spouse is concerned about doing all they can for the other, the relationship thrives.

Another type of relationship where we see this dynamic at play is in the workplace. After all, a job is essentially a relationship between an employer and an employee. Both parties in this relationship also have to understand why they are in it—is it to give or to get?

In Chapter 3, we talked about what it looks like when an employee is in it to get. Obviously, all jobs have a paycheck attached to them. Still, it is easy to tell the difference between an employee who is just doing the minimum to get by and collect that paycheck, and the one who is there with an attitude to deliver more than expected. Here is a different translation of Colossians 3:22-24, the passage quoted in the previous chapter:

Servants, obey your masters in everything. Obey all the time, even when they can't see you. Don't just pretend to work hard so that they will treat you well. No, you must serve your masters honestly because you respect the Lord. In all the work you are given, do the best you can. Work as though you are working for the Lord, not any earthly master. Remember that you will receive your reward from the Lord, who will give you what he promised his people. Yes, you are serving Christ. He is your real Master.[52]

In this passage, we have a picture of both kinds of employees. We have the faker, who kisses up when the boss is around, but then slacks off the moment his back is turned. Then we have the employee who shows integrity and character, doing his or her best when nobody is watching. The first employee is clearly there only to get something, but the second employee is also concerned about giving something. You could call it obedience, honesty, a hard day's work, or a sincere effort, but whatever words you choose, they are all a result of one primary motivating factor: respect.

In this translation of Colossians 3:22-24, Paul is exhorting the members of the church at Colossae to serve their masters honestly, because they "respect the Lord." There is a reward involved in doing so, but they are not being advised to work for the reward itself, but rather for the giver of the reward. Their respect for the Lord is based upon who He is, not what He can do for them.

They are able to have this kind of relationship with God because God has a similar motivation. Because He is God, He doesn't need people to work for Him. He spoke the universe into existence, so

He really doesn't need our help with anything. Instead, God established a relationship with His people based upon what He could do for them. He doesn't want to give us a spiritual paycheck; He wants to invite us into His family!

For this reason, Paul is telling the people to treat their bosses the same way. Respect them for who they are, not for what they can do for you. When you respect someone for the right reasons, the reward comes along with it. In the employer/employee relationship, that reward might take on a tangible appearance, such as in a raise or a bonus. But the real reward is the relationship itself. "While you don't need to suck up to colleagues or flatter them with undeserved compliments, it is important to maintain an atmosphere of politeness, respect, and geniality in order to create an environment where people come in to work with a good attitude."[53]

Respect, or the lack of it, is the confluence of attitude and relationships. A good attitude toward those with whom you have a relationship will earn their respect, and vice versa. The two character traits that will most likely earn this respect are loyalty and a willingness to sacrifice for another's needs. Have you noticed that some of the people you respect the most are the ones who have stuck by you when you were going through a hard time, especially when it was not convenient for them to do so?

A few years ago, there was a woman at our company who was very well respected. She had a great attitude, was a hard worker, and was friendly to everyone. Then she became very ill. She used up all her vacation time and sick time during this illness. But because she had shown loyalty and respect for her co-workers, they returned the favor by offering up some of their own personal time. And since she had also earned the respect of management, the company matched the personal time that her co-workers sacrificed on her behalf. And through this process, I would imagine that she came to appreciate the people that she worked with even more.

So Jesus called the followers together. He said, "You know that the rulers of the non-Jewish people love to show their power over the people. And their important leaders love to use all their authority over the people. But it should not be that way with you. Whoever wants to be your leader must be your servant. Whoever wants to be first must serve the rest of you like a slave. Do as I did: The Son of Man did not come for people to serve him. He came to serve others and to give his life to save many people."[54]

I learned the real meaning of this while on that mission trip in Kenya. We met these awesome guys who were living right there in the slum with the people, ministering to them, basically doing all the things that don't come naturally to people with first-world problems. After the devotional that first morning, they indicated to us that THEY wanted to wash OUR feet. I looked over at my buddy, and he didn't want them to do it. He was shaking his head "no," and the rest of us felt the same way.

Yet, this is precisely the perspective we all need. Jesus knew at the Last Supper that it would indeed be exactly that—his last meal, his last chance for fellowship with His friends. So Jesus, the greatest of all, became the lowest by removing his clothing and tying on a linen towel to wash the feet of His followers. This sort of act was considered by the Jews of that era to be so demeaning that only Gentile slaves would do it. But Jesus did it.

Peter reacted then the same way my companions and I did in Kenya nearly two thousand years later. It just didn't seem right to Peter to be served by the One who was actively healing the world, while he was mostly along for the ride. Jesus' attitude was different though. He was not looking for an opportunity to be served, but to serve and to give an example of serving.

The key words here are "opportunity" and "example." Jesus knew full well that it would be His last night on earth. He made the most of His opportunity to set an example for those who would come after Him. Washing their feet was a very simple act, physically speaking. It didn't take much time or talent and required no treasure at all, but the touch was what mattered. Jesus was more concerned about His disciples relating rightly to each other and in showing them how being respected starts with being respectable. He showed them how to give in a relationship so that they could go and teach others to do likewise. He knew that we would need that teaching.

I wonder if people who lie understand what they're doing. I think some people want grace and certainly they can get grace, but when we lie, we make the people we are lying to feel badly about the relationships and about themselves. We like people who make us feel respected, cared about and honored. Lying to somebody communicates the opposite. [55]

Few things indicate a lack of respect more profoundly than lying to someone. There is, of course, a multitude of reasons why someone might tell a lie. A person may be lying to get out of an awkward situation. Maybe this person has been caught doing something they shouldn't have done. Or perhaps it was a simple mistake that spiraled out of control. When someone asks, "What happened here?" our first instinct is to cover up a mistake by quickly making up a story that will get us out of trouble. Then later on, we tell ourselves, we can "fix things" behind the scenes. No harm done, right?

Except that there is harm when someone who has been lied to finds out about it. Even if the situation that prompted the lie is understandable after it is explained, there remains that stain on the relationship, that nagging doubt that always wonders, "Why didn't they just tell me the truth?" The person who lied didn't mean any disrespect, of course, yet the act of choosing self-preservation over preservation of the relationship, even in the panic of the moment, conveys disrespect just the same.

This level of disrespect can be forgiven easily enough, depending on the strength of the relationship. Deliberate manipulation, however, is another matter entirely. Some people enter into relationships with the sole purpose of using the other person for their own benefit. When these people tell a lie, it is usually with intention, premeditation, and no sense of respect for the other person whatsoever. Liars like that are not interested in what they can put into a relationship. Indeed, they are self-centered to the point where they probably figure that just their mere presence in the relationship is all the contribution that should be required of them.

At age 28, I was named CEO of a small community bank about fifty miles from where I grew up. I quickly made many great friends who I stay in touch with even today. Unfortunately, there were some issues in the loans at the bank. One of my first jobs was to make sure that all loans met or exceeded acceptable credit standards. After being in my new job a couple of months, there was a loan that came across my desk for review. Something just did not smell or look right, and I began to ask lots of questions of the loan officer who had approved and made the loan. He assured me we were well secured and that he had seen the property. The officer was well experienced and probably had aspirations of being in charge of the bank someday.

Because I was new to the area, it was not uncommon for me to get in my car and go look at the real estate we had for collateral. I informed the officer that I wanted to take a look the next day. So the following day, the loan officer and I went to look at the property. I took along a mentor of mine who also served on the board of directors.

But on the way, something happened.

I needed to drop off a check to a local insurance agent with whom I had become great friends. When we stopped at the insurance agent's office, I went in while the loan officer and my mentor stayed in the car. As I entered the office, my friend asked me what I was up to. Before I could say a thing, he noticed the loan officer sitting in my truck and said, "Oh, I know where you are going because your loan officer just called me fifteen minutes ago to find out where the borrower lived."

Now remember, the day before he had told me when questioned about the loan that he had previously inspected the property. So as soon as I heard he had to call to find out where it was, I knew I had been lied to and trust had been broken. But... this story gets better.

We drove out to the property and the loan officer started trying to show me and my mentor where the property lines were. We saw the borrower in the driveway, so I pulled in, got out of the car and introduced myself. I commented that he had a nice place and asked, "How long have you owned the property?"

"I don't own this," he replied. "I just rent it." He went on to tell me that the property we had for collateral was several miles away. I was dismayed to discover that the property we had as collateral was not nearly as valuable as I had been told. We eventually took a small loss on the loan.

But worse than that, the person we were paying to protect our company had lied to me about having inspected the property, and he continued to tell me more lies when describing the property lines. Any trust I had in that employee was broken. I hoped this was all just a one-time mistake. But with my lie-detector radar on full alert, I soon found several other incidents over the next few months, and the loan officer had to be fired.

I have made mistakes. We all do. But there is something we should all learn and remember: "If you mess up, fess up." People will forgive you and trust can be reclaimed.

I often wondered what caused the loan officer to lie. I may never know for sure, but it could have been simple pride, the desire for power or one of several other reasons. But I know this: Whatever it was, he valued it more than he valued relationships and even his job.

So how does this happen? How does someone get to the point of habitually taking advantage of people? It all comes back to what we value most. If we value people and relationships the most, then we will naturally treat people with respect without having to think too much about it. If we value something else more than people—anything else—then respect will erode, and relationships will suffer. This isn't just endemic to chronic liars and manipulators. If we're not careful, any one of us can drift into a pattern of disrespect.

You see, as a communication professor, I preach to my students (and my kids) about "being present." I tell them that most of communication is simply to show the other person that you care, and that they matter to you. How do you do that? By being present. [56]

I'm very concerned about smartphones. You'll recall the statistic in Chapter 2 about how many times a day the average person looks at their phone. If a person says he cares about you and respects you, then he shouldn't be giving you only part of his attention. I've been guilty of this myself. I've gone to dinner with friends and sat there at the table looking at my phone. One night, my wife called me out for checking my phone, and I got mad and tried to make excuses for myself. It didn't seem like that big of a problem to me. But about a week later, we went to dinner with another couple. I counted one of them looking at their phone nine times and the other ten times. We'd be in the middle of a conversation and one of their phones would go off, and they'd say, "Uh, hold on," and then say to each other, "Look at this. So-and-so just texted such-and-such," or "Look what they just posted on Facebook." What does that communicate about our relationship? Did they care what I had to say? Couldn't that call have waited thirty or forty minutes until dinner was over and they were by themselves? After dinner that night when I got in the car, I apologized to my wife and thanked her for pointing out my own phone habit.

Of course, there are exceptions to every rule. If somebod[y]
down and says, "I want to apologize; I have to keep my pho[ne]
for this call from a spouse, or a child, or a co-worker," then e[very]
body understands. But today when I go to dinner with other pe[o]
ple, my phone goes somewhere else. I used to carry my phone int[o]
church, but now when I go to church, my phone stays out in the
car. I don't need to look at it between services; I don't need to look
at it during service. I don't need that distraction. I need to focus
on the moment and learn to be present with people.

> *The greatest gift you can give someone is your time,*
> *your attention, your love, your concern.* [57]

While smartphones definitely can be a problem, they are not THE
problem. They are merely the latest, and perhaps most egregious,
symptom of the problem of our task-oriented culture. There is
nothing wrong with being task-oriented to a certain degree. We all
need to accomplish goals. But it seems the general attitude of our
culture is, "I will have time for you when I am done with this."

In other parts of the world, usually in places that are less techno-
logically advanced, the cultural attitude is the opposite. It is more
like, "I will have time for that when I am finished with you." They
are more relationship-oriented than task-oriented. Deadlines ar-
en't as important to them as quality time is, and the quality of the
time is much more important than the quantity. In some parts of
Africa, for example, time together begins with one person saying,
"I'm here if you're here." Then the other will respond, "I'm here."
They are intentionally starting off the interaction by showing that
they are focusing on being present both in the moment and with
each other. It communicates that they respect each other's time
and value the relationship above anything else that might distract
from their time together. Of course, to be this way all the time in
fast-paced 21st Century America may not be practical, but we can
take steps in that direction. It starts with valuing people above our
stuff and our schedules.

Remember: what we value most, what we truly CARE about, is
what we worship. So what's on our thrones? Sometimes it's simply
our own busyness. We never mean for that to happen, but it's like
a fish that finds itself on a hook. That fish was swimming along,
just living its life, but it got distracted by something shiny, and
that set it on a path it never imagined... with a decidedly unfavor-
able outcome. We're a lot like fish, in that sometimes we find our-

ꝗged off and enticed by the bait of our own desire," ys. We never mean to get caught up in activities ch of our time, but it happens all too easily none- t the only thing we're throwing away, though.

I love you

Back in Chapter 2, we discussed how time is a currency. We all have the same amount of it each day, and it's up to us to choose how we are going to spend it. In Chapter 3, where we talked about attitude, there was another currency present, though not explicitly mentioned. It is the currency of influence. Just as we all begin each day with a certain amount of time, we also have a certain amount of influence ahead of us that day. We will interact with a certain number of people in a variety of ways. Our attitudes in those interactions will determine how this currency of influence is spent or squandered. The knowledge that the currency of our time is fixed and limited each day, and that we also don't know how many more days we have left, should spur us on to develop the attitude of making the most of our currency of influence each day. But how do we do that?

There is a third currency we all have that flows out of the first two: the currency of love. When we value our relationships first, seeking the benefit of others and looking for opportunities to serve, this is how we spend that currency. The more we focus on living out this concept, the more we realize that our stewarding of the currency of love is inextricable from how we manage the other two. We have a limited amount of time to influence those around us by showing them love and respect. Also, as with the other two currencies, the currency of love is meaningless if you don't spend it, as it can't be kept or hoarded.

Perhaps the most significant thing about the currency of love is that it is unlimited. With time, you get twenty-four hours a day, and on the day of your death, your account is maxed out. With influence, you are limited to the number of people with whom you interact. The currency of love, though, pays itself forward with compounding interest. Every act of service that you give is received by someone. That person can then use his or her time and influence to pass on the love you gave, and so on, paying dividends as it goes. This is possible because, while what we do with our time and influence depends upon us, love doesn't, because it didn't start with us.

We love because God loved us first.[58]

God loved the world this way: He gave his only Son so that everyone who believes in Him will not die but will have eternal life.[59]

The only reason that we are capable of loving in the first place is because we have been loved by God, who is the source of love. He demonstrated this to us by sacrificing His only Son for us. In doing this, the example was set for all time that love involves sacrifice and the attitude of putting the other party of a relationship first. God, who is above all, put us first by sending Jesus to die for us.

We will never be in a position to make a sacrifice that great for a cause that momentous. Nevertheless, we have been given a pattern to follow. This is a pattern of selflessness, in which we seek practical ways to put others first. Chapter 13 of 1 Corinthians lists many characteristics of selfless love. Among these are patience, kindness, an absence of envy, humility, a servant attitude, calmness, forgiveness, justice, truth, endurance, trust, and hope. These are the traits we must nurture. Since we are imperfect beings, though, we are certainly not going to succeed in this endeavor all the time. So what happens when we fail?

I am learning that relationships are like cars—from time to time they break down. If I ignore the regular maintenance of relational repair it will be to my peril. Marriage, parenting, work, family and friends all require ongoing evaluation and consistent investment of time and energy. It is especially necessary for me to prayerfully look for ways to serve those whom I have hurt or have hurt me. Relational repair doesn't mean a perfect relationship, but one that applies love to the wound.[60]

In Luke 10:30-37, Jesus tells a parable about a man who is beaten, robbed, and left for dead by the side of the road. A couple of holy men see him lying there, but are too busy to help, so they pass by. Then a Samaritan stops to help, takes him to an inn and even provides financially for his care when he has to leave.

The historical context of the parable is important. Samaria was founded in 885 BC by Omri, king of Israel. By this time, Israel had split into a northern kingdom and a southern kingdom, called

Judah. 1 Kings 16:25 states that, "Omri did more evil in the sight of the Lord than all who were before him." It went downhill from there. About 150 years later, Samaria fell to Assyrian conquerors. The defeated Israelites intermarried with the Assyrians, much to the consternation of the Jews in the southern kingdom, who strove to maintain their historical and racial identity as God's chosen people. This enmity between the Jews and Samaria culminated when the Samaritans built their own temple on Mt. Gerizim to rival the temple in Jerusalem. This hatred had continued unabated for seven centuries and was still firmly entrenched in the minds of those hearing Jesus tell this parable.

The point is that the Samaritan in the parable wasn't just a generally nice guy. He was a member of a group that had been considered no better than animals for nine hundred years by the group to which the beaten man belonged. The Samaritan wasn't just helping someone in need. He was making a conscious and very difficult decision to show love to someone who on any other day would have shown nothing but hatred and derision toward him. The Samaritan made the most of his opportunity to stop the erosion of the relationship between their nations by serving without prejudice.

Therefore, if you are bringing an offering to God and you remember that your brother is angry at you or holds a grudge against you, then leave your gift before the altar, go to your brother, repent and forgive one another, be reconciled, and then return to the altar to offer your gift to God.[61]

The first step in fixing a broken relationship is humility. When we are angry at someone, it is easy to slip into an attitude of unforgiveness, as though the person we are mad at doesn't even deserve to be forgiven. But what if that person feels the same way about us? If we have cultivated an attitude of respect toward our fellow human beings, then it should not take long for us to recall the inherent worth that another person has. If our motivation of being in a relationship with that person is to give, then whatever the other person has done to make us upset should not be of primary importance. We need to get down to the business of giving.

The Samaritan in the story did this by seeing a specific need and meeting it without dwelling on his issues with Jews in general. When we set our grievances aside, small ones or large ones, and focus on helping and serving, those grievances tend to stay to the side where we left them, because when we are helping someone out, we only see the person, not the offense.

While it is exceedingly difficult to have respect for someone who has offended you, that obstacle is removed once you set the offense itself aside and focus on serving. That's where the healing begins.

Whoever forgives an offense seeks love, but whoever keeps bringing up the issue separates the closest of friends.[62]

The restoration of trust and intimacy in a relationship brings along with it the restoration of respect. Trust and offense cannot exist in the same relationship at the same time. You just have to decide which one is more important to you.

Holding grudges erodes trust. It's as simple as that. What happens in your mind is that a grudge begins to take on a life of its own, a life that becomes much more insistent than the original offense ever was. Soon you may find yourself not wanting to trust the other person with something that doesn't even relate to the original offense, because all you can think about is how mad at him or her you are.

Healing in a relationship begins with a simple choice: you need to make the decision to seek reconciliation. You do this by choosing to believe the best about that person rather than expecting the worst. There is always risk with trust. You may get burned again. You may get betrayed. You cannot afford, however, to get hung up on what MAY happen. Healing and reconciliation aren't ever going to occur until somebody makes the first move. So which somebody is going to go first?

Somebody should have done the job And Everybody should have, But in the end Nobody did What Anybody could have.[63]

Don't wait. Take responsibility for the relationship and be the peacemaker. Above all, be transparent about the part you played in the damage done to the relationship. It's all about accountability. When you are in a relationship, the other person has the right to hold you accountable, like my wife did when I was looking at my smartphone too much. If you want the other person to trust you, then you have to be real about your failings. Most of the time, when the other person witnesses this authenticity coming from you, they will be inclined to reciprocate. This technique won't work every time, but it will more often than not. When you stretch out the olive branch first, you are demonstrating that you respect the relationship. If the other person refuses it, then that's their problem. You have done your part.

The important thing is to DO your part. Spend your currency of love extravagantly. But make sure that you are also spending it wisely. It's important to reach out to people with whom we have gotten sideways in a relationship, but this does not mean that we should put ourselves in a position where people can hurt us repeatedly. There is a difference between being humble and being a doormat. If the person with whom you are seeking reconciliation has a history of being in relationships to get, then you must proceed with caution and have a clear set of boundaries in mind. They may only be interested in manipulating you or establishing power over you.

Remember, you deserve respect too!

To laugh often and love much;
To win the respect of intelligent people
And the affection of children;
To earn the approbation of honest critics
And endure the betrayal of false friends;
To appreciate beauty;
To find the best in others; To give one's self;
To leave the world a little better, Whether by a healthy child,
A garden patch,
Or a redeemed social condition;
To have played and laughed with enthusiasm
And sung with exaltation;
To know even one life has breathed easier
Because you have lived. . . .

This is to have succeeded.

—*Ralph Waldo Emerson*

So far, we have asked the questions, "What do you CARE about?" and "How do your choices reflect that you CARE?" We have used these questions to discern our calling and reveal our attitudes. In this chapter, we talked about respect and relationships. We have covered the what, the why, and the who. Now it's time to talk about the how.

CARE EXCELLENCE

"Adequacy is the enemy of excellence."
—Peter Drucker

What is excellence? If you look in a dictionary or thesaurus, you'll find words such as "superiority," "preeminence," "transcendence," "distinction," "merit," and "virtue." But what is it really?

For the purposes of this book, excellence is putting the finishing touches on showing people that you CARE. Whenever you have the right attitude, and the proper respect for the people with whom you are interacting, you're naturally going to do things with excellence, because you know deep down that putting forth a half-hearted effort doesn't show that you CARE about others, your work, or yourself.

Near enough is not good enough, therefore good enough
is not near enough, and only your best will do.

The people that I always remember are the ones who do things with excellence. Over the years, I have managed a lot of people in a lot of different places. The ones I remember the most are the people I knew I could depend on to get things done, to get them done right, and to get them done right away. If I ever have a choice between two people to take care of something, the one who has shown me that he or she will get it done with excellence is the one that will be entrusted with that responsibility. This is also the one I will remember when the time for reviews, raises, or bonuses comes around. They are the people who have good attitudes and do their work with excellence, which earns them my respect.

I have been blessed to work with many people who have these qualities.

In 2001, I was asked to take on a new responsibility of running a small life insurance company. I knew very little about a life insurance company or the industry, but always believed that if I asked the right questions, to the right person, I would get to the right answer. So I accepted the position and moved two states away to a place where I knew absolutely no one.

I was blessed to meet someone who not only knew how to get things done and get them done on time, but also became a great friend and brother in Christ, Ted Miller. Ted is a guy who is humble, loves people, delivers more than is expected and is honest to the bone.

About six months into my new position, the company was not doing very well, and we were just getting to know each other. I remember looking at Ted one day and asking him, "You don't know why Jess Correll pays me what he does, do you?"

Ted, because of who he was, looked at me, his boss, and said, "No, I don't." I assured Ted that if the company was not performing the way we thought it should in two years, I would find something else to do because I would not take my pay without delivering the excellence that was expected. Praise God, the company did turn around, because I loved what I did.

How does this relate to excellence? People like Ted will tell you the truth, even if it affects them negatively. It was risky for him to tell me I wasn't earning the salary I was paid. But he cared about doing the right things for the right reasons. I knew I could count on him to always perform any duty with excellence.

> *Bondservants, obey your earthly masters with fear and*
> *trembling, with a sincere heart, as you would Christ, not by the*
> *way of eye-service, as people-pleasers, but as bondservants of*
> *Christ, doing the will of God from the heart, rendering service*
> *with a good will as to the Lord and not to man, knowing that*
> *whatever good anyone does, this he will receive back*
> *from the Lord, whether he is a bondservant or is free.*[64]

Just as Paul wrote to the Colossians, he also exhorted the church at Ephesus to do their work as though Jesus Himself were signing their paychecks.

What happens if you work for a boss or a manager who is not Christ-like? Does that give you a free pass from doing your best work? By no means. The point of working with excellence is not to curry favor with your boss and buck for a promotion. If the excellence of your work is not a natural extension of the excellence of your character, the falseness will show. And if you can't hide that falseness from your boss, how much less can you put one over on God?

It's all about your motivation. Are you doing your best in order to get something for yourself, or is it because that's just who you are?

> *Integrity is doing the right thing,*
> *even when no one is watching.*[65]

Cultivating an attitude of respect begins with humility before authority. All authority comes from God. But if we focus on the objects of authority—flawed human beings—then it is easy for us to become discouraged. Why should we go to the trouble of respecting people who don't respect us? If you have ever had teenage children in your home, you have probably had that question flung in your direction a time or two.

If you focus on the One who gives all authority, though, you will give your best effort to every endeavor. By counting your relationship with God as more important than any reward—by showing that you CARE—you develop excellence as a habit.

On the other hand, a prideful, self-centered attitude will make you naturally contradictory to authority, which will also show through in your work. Malachi 1:6-8 illustrates what this looks like in the context of worship:

The Lord of Heaven's Armies says to the priests:
"A son honors his father, and a servant respects his master.
If I am your father and master, where are the honor and r
espect I deserve? You have shown contempt for my name!

"But you ask, 'How have we ever shown contempt for your name?'
You have shown contempt by offering defiled sacrifices on my altar.
Then you ask, 'How have we defiled the sacrifices?'

"You defile them by saying the altar of the Lord deserves no respect.
When you give blind animals as sacrifices, isn't that wrong?
And isn't it wrong to offer animals that are crippled and diseased?
Try giving gifts like that to your governor, and see how pleased
he is!" says the Lord of Heaven's Armies.[66]

The priests of this era had been so lackadaisical concerning their duties for such a longtime that they didn't even seem to be aware of their half-hearted worship. God, through His prophet Malachi, said that their actions demonstrated that they do not CARE about Him. They were going through the motions of doing their priestly duties, but they didn't have respect for their Master, and their relationship with Him had been damaged as a result.

The same thing can happen in our lives and in our workplaces, if we're not careful. If we are not focused on giving our best, we can fall into a rut of just showing up every day at work, clocking in on time, doing the minimum to get by, clocking out on time, and continuing to ride that merry-go-round until payday. Employees like this try to keep a low profile and not do anything that will get them noticed. Ironically, efforts NOT to be set apart can set someone apart for the wrong reasons if their co-workers are doing their best and they notice someone who is not. People who are just going through the motions at their workplace might actually find themselves singled out for poor performance, even if they haven't committed any gross infractions, simply because they aren't giving their best.

Be a yardstick of quality. Some people aren't used
to an environment where excellence is expected.[67]

72

So how do we go about living our lives with excellence from day to day? What does it look like? Some other "e"-words can give us insight into how to make excellence a reality for us individually.

Example

I have given you this as an example
so that you may do as I have done.[68]

Jesus Christ set the example for us by providing a pattern of behavior for us to model.

He already knew what His calling was as a 12-year-old. He had the attitude of being a servant rather than being served. He gave the sick and lowly dignity and respect through His healing miracles and a willingness to cross social boundaries. And He provided the ultimate example of giving one's best by sacrificing Himself on the cross for the benefit of all humanity.

Expectations

When you're doing something with excellence, you don't do it from an expectation of personal gain. For example, Christ gave us the command to love one another. He never said, "Love one another IF they love you back," or, "Love one another IF they're going to help you get a bonus or raise." He said, "Love one another."

Excellence is the same way. There are no "ifs." You have to remember to ask yourself, "Why am I in this relationship? For what I can give, or for what I can get?" And if you decide you're going to do things with excellence, you're going to be willing to give, and you're going to be a better person for it.

Our message to you is true, our motives are pure,
our conduct is absolutely above board. We speak under
the solemn sense of being trusted by God with the Gospel.
We do not aim to please men, but to please God who knows us
through and through. No one could ever say, as again you know,
that we used flattery to conceal greedy motives, and God
himself is witness to our honesty. We made no attempt to win
honor from men, either from you or from anybody else, though
I suppose as Christ's own messengers we might have done so.[69]

Paul's message to the church at Thessalonica illustrates the attitude that he and the other apostles had—to focus their efforts not on a reward, but on God, the ultimate giver of their ultimate reward. They wanted to please God because He knew them "through and through." The respect they had for their relationship with God was demonstrated by the excellence of character they displayed in their interactions with the Thessalonians.

Setting goals is a very useful tool where productivity is concerned, but it can backfire if we try to misuse excellence in an attempt to plan our future. If we are giving our best with the expectation of a reward, such as a promotion, then we are going about our business with the wrong motivation for two reasons.

First, by trying to impress authority figures with our excellence, we are actually trying to manipulate them into giving us what we want. We turn the relationship into one that is focused on getting, not giving.

Second, we are losing sight of the fact that promotions aren't ultimately up to us.

> *For promotion and power come from nowhere on earth,*
> *but only from God. He promotes one and deposes another.*[70]

If we are focused on the promotion or reward itself, then we start to expect it. Then, when the reward doesn't come or we are passed over for the promotion, we may react with resentfulness. If our motivations are wrong and we develop wrong expectations as a result, we can inflate our sense of self-importance. This can very easily lead to damaged relationships, particularly with the people who end up getting whatever it was we had set ourselves up to expect that we were going to get.

This is why it is so important to focus on what you're giving and to have faith that your efforts are being noticed, if not by people, then at least by God. If you are convinced that He is the one who gives any reward worth having, then you can take comfort in knowing that you will be lifted up to just the right place at just the right time.

Encouragement

Encouraging other people takes effort, but a little can go a long way. I know that when I've gone through some trials, the loss of a parent for example, it really meant a lot when I got notes that said, "Hey, I'm thinking about you," or "Praying for you."

Words have so much power. We don't go through a single day, even a single hour, without recalling words that have been spoken to us, whether recently or long ago. Our motivations for doing just about anything come from responding to words we have heard. When people are on the receiving end of hurtful and negative speech, they either choose to believe it and let it tear them down, or else they choose not to believe it, and exhaust their energy trying to prove the person wrong. Have you found yourself doing either of these recently? Chances are, if you're around other people much, you have.

But there's another way to go about this. What if we used our words to build up instead of to tear down? Paul said to the believers at Ephesus, "Let everything you say be good and helpful, so that your words will be an encouragement to those who hear them."[71]

For many of us, this is hard, but as we move through the progression of finding our calling, adjusting our attitudes, and learning respect, we are renewing our minds and pointing ourselves toward excellence. What is going on inside us will reflect on the outside, because "out of the abundance of the heart, the mouth speaks."[72]

A substantial component of encouragement is showing respect by listening. To effectively encourage people with your words, you have to know what their needs are, so you can build them up in accordance with those needs. The only way to discover what those needs are is to listen. Remember when we talked earlier about how our attitude impacts others like ripples on a pond? Encouragement does the same thing. Anyone close to the person you are encouraging may directly hear or hear about your words and be encouraged themselves. Maybe they are going through the same type of problem, or perhaps they might be inspired enough by your example to pay it forward and go encourage someone else.

Words can build you up
Words can break you down;
Start a fire in your heart or
Put it out.[73]

Again: Encouragement takes effort. It is an investment of energy into a relationship. Like any investment, there is no return without a deposit. Encouragement requires putting the interests of others ahead of your own. Of course, if you have already cultivated an attitude of respect in your relationships, you're halfway there.

Enthusiasm

It is very unusual to find excellence where there is no enthusiasm. Giving your best is exceedingly difficult without excitement or a sense of enjoyment in fulfilling your purpose.

Anything you have a burning passion for, you are very likely to do with excellence. But to have lasting enthusiasm, the first thing you need is an awareness of the importance of your passion.

To the one who spoke and set the sun ablaze
To the one who stopped the storm and walked the waves
To the one who took the tree so He could say
You matter, I hope you know you matter.[74]

Remember the movie, *It's a Wonderful Life?* Jimmy Stewart played George Bailey, a man whose life didn't go the way he had planned. One Christmas, as everything starts to unravel, he decides to take his own life. However, he is rescued by an angel who shows him what life in his town would have been like had he never been born. When George sees the significance of his existence, and how he has affected the lives of so many people in his town, he sees the light and rushes home to his family. No one can deny that the closing scenes of this movie are filled with enthusiasm, both for the Christmas season, and for life itself.

So how wonderful is your life? Do you ever stop to think about how you have influenced the people with whom you have come into contact over the years? It is always a good idea to count your blessings, but have you ever stopped to consider the ways in which you are a blessing to others?

What you do matters and what you say matters. Not just the content, but the enthusiasm behind it. Inspirational speaker Barbara Glanz writes a blog titled, "Spreading Contagious Enthusiasm." She has traveled the world, speaking in all fifty states and on all seven continents (yes, even Antarctica) telling stories of people she has encountered who have made a difference in their workplaces with their enthusiasm. Glanz explains her motto this way: "I say to managers, 'Are you contagiously enthusiastic about the importance of the work you're doing? Because if you're not, how do you expect the employees to be?' I talk about that every time I speak. Some people see that as fluff, I think. But it's passion and about feeling your work at the heart level."[75]

Glanz had the opportunity to live out this concept when she gave a half-day presentation on customer service to the Singapore Security Police. These were hardened, middle-aged men who were used to having absolute power and were not easily impressed. The day was not going well for Glanz at first. She relates what she did to turn things around:

"About an hour into the presentation, I just stopped and said to them, 'Can you tell how much I believe in what I'm sharing with you today? This isn't a presentation, and it isn't a job to me. It's how I try to live my life.' And it was like the floodgates opened. At the end of the day, these guys stayed for hours on their own time. They all wanted their pictures taken with me and wanted me to sign their books . . . They may not agree with everything I said, but they respected how much I believed in what I was saying."[76]

Just as with encouragement, enthusiasm also takes effort. It's easy for a routine to become a rut, and the temptation to slack off is always with us. However, if we are continuously aware of our attitudes, we all have the ability to see our work for what it is truly worth and approach it with enthusiasm.

Efficiency

If you are inefficient, you have a right to be afraid of the consequences.[77]

Our expectations are directly linked to our efficiency. If we are in a relationship expecting to get, our self-centeredness and inward focus will eventually result in a decline in motivation when we don't get what we want. As motivation erodes, so does our efficiency, and that certainly doesn't lead anywhere good.

On the other hand, a person committed to excellence puts a premium on doing things right the first time. Such people are already in the mindset of giving their best in order to enrich the lives of others. A person committed to excellence demonstrates efficiency by following through, paying attention to detail, persevering under pressure and meeting deadlines.

"Gentlemen, we are going to relentlessly chase perfection, knowing full well we will not catch it, because nothing is perfect. But we are going to relentlessly chase it, because in the process we will catch excellence. I am not remotely interested in just being good."[78]

Vince Lombardi said these words in his first team meeting as the coach of the Green Bay Packers in 1959. It is important how he made the distinction between perfection and excellence. In the same way, I want to make it clear that efficiency does not mean perfection either.

Perfection is not attainable, but efficiency is.

Where perfection is getting everything exactly right, efficiency also involves getting things done. Efficiency has a balance in it where you are making steady progress toward your goal, but also crossing the t's and dotting the i's as you go. You can't go too quickly, or you will miss important details. Then you will spend four to five times the time and effort going back to fix your errors as you would have spent if you had just done it right the first time.
On the other hand, if you're so focused on perfection that you lose sight of the goal of completion, then you will end up slowing down the process to a point where the job never seems to get done.
People who take too long to get things done produce nothing. Yet, people who get things done too quickly waste a lot of time because they have to go back over their work and fix things.

So efficiency, this sweet spot in the middle, is where we want to be. Our work is accurate, but it is also completed in an amount of time that frees us up to think more and do more.

I knew I could control one thing, and that is my time and my hours and my effort and my efficiency.[79]

The biggest reason that perfection is not attainable is that none of us is perfect.

Efficiency does not demand perfection, but excellence prescribes that we should do the best we can with what we have. Consider this exchange between God and Moses at the burning bush in the desert near Mt. Sinai:

> But Moses said to God, "Who am I that I should go to Pharaoh and bring the Israelites out of Egypt?"
>
> And God said, "I will be with you. And this will be the sign to you that it is I who have sent you: When you have brought the people out of Egypt, you will worship God on this mountain."
>
> Moses answered, "What if they do not believe me or listen to me and say, 'The Lord did not appear to you'?"
>
> Then the Lord said to him, "What is that in your hand?"
>
> "A staff," he replied.
>
> The Lord said, "Throw it on the ground." Moses threw it on the ground and it became a snake, and he ran from it.
>
> Then the Lord said to him, "Reach out your hand and take it by the tail." So Moses reached out and took hold of the snake and it turned back into a staff in his hand.
>
> Moses said to the Lord, "Pardon your servant, Lord. I have never been eloquent, neither in the past nor since you have spoken to your servant. I am slow of speech and tongue."
>
> The Lord said to him, "Who gave human beings their mouths? Who makes them deaf or mute? Who gives them sight or makes them blind? Is it not I, the Lord? Now go; I will help you speak and will teach you what to say."[80]

In this passage, God has just asked Moses to return to Egypt after being away for forty years, to deliver the Israelites from bondage under Pharaoh. You can tell that Moses is not excited about this plan by the excuses he makes. This isn't because he wants to be disobedient to God; he just doesn't feel he has what it takes to get the job done. Moses seems to feel that the perfect God who is speaking to him would naturally demand perfection when setting him to a task. Yet, God isn't actually doing that. He meets Moses right where he is, with all his insecurities and inadequacies, be they real or perceived, and asks him one question: "What's in your hand?" God is asking that question both literally (referring to the staff) and figuratively.

He is asking Moses to take inventory of what he has to work with. It's kind of a trick question, though, because what He really wants Moses to say is that he has the power of God in his hand. God displays that graphically by turning the staff into a snake, but He really seems to want Moses to believe without seeing. Most of all, He's trying to get across to Moses that He isn't asking for perfection. All Moses needs to do is be efficient in following directions and speaking the words he is given to speak.

All of us have encountered the same fear of failure. Sometimes we just want to do everything perfectly because we are perfectionists; however, many times this fear comes from how we imagine others will perceive our apparent failures. I'm not talking as much about facing punishment or derision from others so much as falling into the trap of becoming a people-pleaser. Of course, there is nothing inherently wrong with wanting to make people happy.

However, if you measure the worth of your work by how you believe it makes other people feel about you as a person, then you have made yourself a slave, not only to those people you are trying so desperately to impress, but also to perfectionism itself.

Efficiency, then, is neither expecting perfection nor settling for "good enough." It's when you have resolved in your mind you are going to continue looking for better ways to do things, ways to work smarter rather than harder. A mind set on efficiency will lead to a lifestyle of. . .

Effectiveness

*Efficiency is doing things right;
effectiveness is doing the right things.*[81]

You may be uniquely skilled at bringing a certain task or process to completion, on time, and with a high degree of accuracy. However, if the task you have completed with such efficiency isn't the one you were supposed to be doing, then the efficiency doesn't matter, because you have missed the mark on effectiveness.

For example, you might be the pride of your online gaming community, because of the speed and alacrity with which you can capture the flag while playing Call of Duty. However, if you were supposed to be studying for your final exams when you were playing video games, does it really matter that your team tasted victory because of your performance on the virtual battlefield? If studying should have been your priority, then you have not made an effective use of your time.

Back in Chapter 3, we noted that living your calling effectively involves your attitude meeting your aptitude. We do tend to have the greatest efficiency where we have the greatest proficiency, but effectiveness requires us to also maintain the attitude of keeping our eyes fixed on the goal, whether that is a short-term goal, or the big-picture goal of living out our calling.

Effectiveness involves self-discipline. To make sure we are doing the right things, we need to continually evaluate how we spend our time and whether our efforts are bearing fruit. Management consultant and author Peter Drucker explains the approach an effective person has when evaluating the tasks on his agenda:

> *"Is this still worth doing?" And if it isn't, he gets rid of it so as to be able to concentrate on the few tasks that, if done with excellence, will really make a difference in the results of his own job and in the performance of his organization.*[82]

This sounds simple enough, but a potential problem with downsizing your task list is the possibility of monotony creeping in. Sometimes the most worthwhile activity is not the one that is the most fun. You could find yourself doing something important, but all the while wishing you were doing something else. Having a good attitude about your work at the start is usually easy enough; however, maintaining effectiveness until the job's completion requires.

Endurance

> *We must not get tired of doing good. We will receive our harvest of eternal life at the right time. We must not give up. When we have the opportunity to do good to anyone, we should do it.*[83]

No matter what our character is like, or how excited we are about the idea of living out our calling, it is difficult to persevere in having the proper attitude for the duration of a long project, especially if it involves a lot of repetitive work, day in and day out. If we don't see immediate results from our labors we may become impatient, putting ourselves in danger of thinking our work is less valuable than it actually is, or that we aren't ever going to benefit from it. Over time, we might experience a shift in our attitude from giving to getting and consequently begin to develop unrealistic expectations of how we ought to be rewarded for our work. We might start saying to ourselves, "I deserve a break," or a treat, or some TV time, or whatever it is we would rather be doing at that moment instead of working. Remember, though, that a life of excellence does not focus on short-term rewards. Excellence is a commitment, and commitments require endurance. Sometimes endurance is painful.

But you, remain steady in every situation, endure suffering, do the work that a proclaimer of the Good News should, and do everything your service to God requires.

For as for me, I am already being poured out on the altar; yes, the time for my departure has arrived. I have fought the good fight, I have finished the race, I have kept the faith. All that awaits me now is the crown of righteousness which the Lord, "the Righteous Judge," will award to me on that Day — and not only to me, but also to all who have longed for him to appear.[84]

Endurance is the product of keeping your eyes on the goal and not being distracted by the James 1:14 fishhooks we talked about in the last chapter. Some temptations we can physically put away, like television, video games, or smartphones. Sometimes it's a matter of mindset—making the decision that the distraction is not as important as the goal.

Life, however, sometimes has other plans. It throws things at us that we are not expecting, or could not prepare for, such as the illness or death of a loved one, a job loss, a medical emergency, or a natural disaster. In cases like these, the "distraction" becomes the priority, at least for a time. Perseverance is necessary during these trials to maintain our integrity. Even when we are in survival mode, living from one day to the next, or even from one minute to the next, it is still vital to maintain the faithfulness to follow through with what we say we will do and to finish what we start.

We may have to adjust our timetable, perhaps more than once, but any goal worth setting is a goal worth achieving.

Another thing that needs to be adjusted in times of trouble is our standard of excellence. It's still important that we do our best at all times, but some days, our best is going to be better than other days. For example, if someone that I am managing is going through some trials, and their focus can't be 100 percent on their work, I understand that their level of excellence is going to drop for a bit. The important thing in the long term is that the level comes back up once the storm passes. That's all people can expect from each other, and it's really all we can expect from ourselves. If people know what you're going through, then they should understand you're doing the best you can with whatever you're dealing with on that day.

Extra

More than any of the other "e-words" that we have discussed, the word "extra" is probably the one that best sums up a life lived with excellence. Extra means going above and beyond, delivering more than what is expected, standing out. A person who gives extra effort is going to be noticed and remembered. For example, a mechanic who fixes your car and hands you the bill has done his job. But a mechanic who tells you when the job will be done, gives you his own car to drive if yours doesn't get fixed on time, then lowers your bill because it turned out to be higher than the original estimate—that's the mechanic that you're going to tell your friends about. Because he delivered more than you expected, he's most likely going to get your business again the next time you need a mechanic.

Extra is the opposite of "good enough." A person who runs his car through an automatic car wash gets the dirt and grime off, and that's good enough. The car is clean. But a person who hand-washes and hand-waxes his car is going to have a vehicle that gets noticed.

My point is not that it should be your goal to be noticed because of your appearance or material possessions. I am merely pointing out that the results of extra effort will draw people's attention, whereas the results of a "good enough" effort likely won't.

Developing the habit of giving extra when you feel good will pay dividends when you find yourself compelled to do something you'd rather not be doing. You've heard the phrase, "Go the extra mile?" That sounds like an encouragement to simply have a good attitude, and that is part of it. This phrase actually has its origin in the Sermon on the Mount:

If anybody forces you to go a mile with him,
do more—go two miles with him.[85]

The "anybody" Jesus referred to in that place and time was a Roman soldier. The Romans practiced impressment, which meant soldiers had the authority to command any civilian to carry his gear for a mile. So when Jesus talks about going the extra mile, it's not a pep talk. It's about giving more than expected, even under duress. The audience to which Jesus was speaking was an oppressed and occupied people. Jesus isn't just telling them to obey the soldiers out of respect for their position or fear of punishment for disobedience. He is encouraging them to show their character by making a sacrifice to provide something extra.

Jesus, of course, made the ultimate sacrifice, and gave the ultimate "extra," by dying on the cross for our sins. He gave us His very best under the very worst of circumstances. By doing so, He showed us the best possible example of how to CARE. Our response, then, is to seek to give our best in all circumstances, because a life of excellence honors God and inspires others to CARE as well.

The difference between ordinary and
extraordinary is that little extra.
—Jimmy Johnson

CARE ENOUGH TO DARE ENOUGH

As long as you're green, you're growing.
As soon as you're ripe, you start to rot.[86]

I remember graduating from high school and making the decision not to go to college.

To be honest, I was tired of books. I thought, "I'm never going to read another book. I'm done." That was a foolish thought. Today I love books. I read as many books as I can, because I want to be green and growing, not ripe and rotting. I think that going down this journey to find out what your calling is—to find your purpose—is really just a journey to continue to be green and growing. I sincerely hope this book has helped you ask the right questions in order to answer your main question: "What is my calling?" My goal in writing this was not so much to direct people to their calling, but to give them the tools to direct themselves.

No matter where we are in life, there's still work for us to do. We shouldn't ever be afraid to try new things just because we're comfortable doing what we've always done. Sometimes our calling simply means doing something new in the same place, but sometimes it can mean going somewhere far beyond our comfort zone—either mentally, spiritually, physically, or perhaps a combination of all those. If we have the attitude of being green and growing, our eyes will stay open for opportunities to put our plans into action, for new people to meet with new points of view that sharpen us, and for new and better ways to do things we are already doing.

The most important thing to remember about being green and growing is that we should never have the attitude that we have "arrived." There is always still something we can do to show that we CARE. So, if one calling in your life has been fulfilled, that's a good indicator that another one is on the way. Staying focused on your calling acts as a compass for your life. It keeps you on track so you don't drift, as we are all tempted to do.

Nothing to it but to do it

Happy is the person who can hold up under the trials of life.
At the right time, he'll know God's sweet approval and
will be crowned with life. As God has promised,
the crown awaits all who love Him.[87]

We show an unbelieving world the love of Jesus when we show we CARE. Many people want to do something positive in the world but don't know what to do or how to go about doing it. It is so easy to be overwhelmed by options or just the sheer weight of the need in the world.

It is also easy to become apathetic and think that nothing you do will make a difference in this big world. Many of us mean well but just get so busy and distracted that we never get around to doing what we would like to do.

There's nothing to it but to DO it, and that means first we must start. So, this is my challenge to you: START TODAY. By no means will you automatically have the answers right away, as if by magic. A journey does involve movement, however, and movement involves a first step.

What's the first step? I would suggest, before trying to figure out where you're going, it would be a good idea to have a clear understanding of where you are. Keeping in mind the principles you have learned in this book, take a look at yourself and your life-style. How would you like your life to be different?

The next step is to start asking questions. This may be uncomfort-able at first, but find some people whom you know will give you honest feedback and ask them for some ways you can improve yourself. Remember, you will probably have to use the three-ques-tion technique we mentioned in Chapter 3 to get to an honest answer. The purpose of asking these questions is to solidify in your mind what it is about yourself or your lifestyle that you need to change to find and live your calling. The beginning of showing people you CARE is simply finding those first couple of things to change. Remember, this is a journey. Journeys don't happen all at once.

A journey of a thousand miles begins with a single step.
—Lao-tzu, The Tao Te Ching

Like any journey worth taking, this one will not be without its challenges. This isn't exactly a "normal" thing you're about to do. Many people want to know what their calling or purpose is, but few actually try to find it. When those who don't follow through see that you are doing that, you should anticipate some pushback from them. Because if you are putting the principles in this book to use, then you will be seeking your calling for the glory of God and the betterment of others.

The world doesn't operate that way. Our culture trains us from birth to be either self-sufficient and ambitious, or else entitled and lazy. Interdependence and hard work are not valued as they once were; however, they are still as *valuable* as they have ever been. We live in an age where "good enough" is good enough and comfort is king. I hope you realize by now, though, that this kind of atti-tude will never get you where you want to go.

Talking about change won't get it done. Neither will reading this book and thinking to yourself, "Those are some great ideas. I'll have to take that under advisement." CARE requires action. And as your actions ripple into the world around you, who knows how many other people will get the itch to start doing something as well? Don't concern yourself with the "how many," though. Let it be enough to know that some will.

You are not alone

The just care for the cause of the poor;
the wicked do not understand such care.[88]

Understand something: there are going to be days, quite a few of them in fact, when you're simply not going to feel like dealing with this. You will look at people around you who are having a good time while you're giving up your leisure time to devote it to a cause, and you may find yourself questioning your decision to follow this path. When those times come, ask yourself this question instead: "At the end of my life, which emotion will be stronger, the enjoyment I felt when watching the season premiere of that TV show (or whatever it is you'd rather be doing), or the regret I will feel for the opportunity I missed to help someone?"

Some days your path will be a lonely one. This is why it is important to build relationships with people who are going the same way you're going in life. If you don't have that, then your emotions can lead you back into your comfort zone—the place where you follow people who do things that make them feel good in the moment. But if those people aren't going the direction you want to go, then following them will get you further and further off course. You can always correct your course, obviously, but why make it more difficult than it has to be?

Whoever you are, there is some younger person who thinks
you are perfect. There is some work that will never be done
if you don't do it. There is someone who would miss you if
you were gone. There is a place that you alone can fill.[89]

Never forget that you are here for a reason. Several reasons, most likely. Sometimes, it isn't even about showing the world the results you got through your own perseverance.

Sometimes it's the act of persevering in and of itself that captures someone's attention. This is especially true for children.

Of course, not everyone reading this book has children, but you're all going to encounter kids at some point. They are always watching. They may not always say so, but they can generally spot a fake person as keenly as adults can, if not more so. What they lack is the life experience and wisdom to figure out how to apply their observations of other people to their own lives. For that reason, I would challenge you to share the ideas in this book with your kids (or someone else's kids, if you don't have any of your own). The principles in this book are intended to lead *anyone* to a more fulfilling life. Why not start early? These values are not generally taught in the public schools, so it's up to us to pass on this wisdom.

So many kids seem completely checked out today, wrapped up in social media, video games, and pop culture. It seems a gargantuan task even to make a teenager aware that a world exists outside of his or her smartphone. What parent these days has not lamented the difficulty of getting their kids to do what's expected of them? I would like to offer a different perspective: Kids do indeed do what's expected of them, but in a different way. I'm not talking about cleaning their rooms or taking out the garbage. I'm talking about a big-picture expectation for their lives.

Expect the best and you will see it

We have a choice in how we relate to other people. We can either believe the best about them or expect the worst from them. Believing the best requires forbearance, forgiveness, and optimism. This tactic encourages and inspires people to try their best to live up to your best expectations. However, the reverse is also true. If you expect the worst from someone, you generally receive that. If your attitude toward the other person is that failure is virtually guaranteed, what incentive are you giving that person to succeed? People are like rivers in that they tend to take the path of least resistance. As such, a person from whom you expect the worst might find it less trouble to fail and get it over with than to try to prove you wrong by excelling. This is especially true with children. They feed on encouragement and wither under criticism. Of course, part of our job as parents is to help our children mature into adults who can do the right thing just because it's right, and let criticism roll off their backs. But that doesn't happen all at once. Kids want to know, which means they have to *hear* that they're doing a good job right now.

It is important to teach kids how to CARE. For older kids, reading this book might help. For younger ones, watching you live a life based on these principles provides an example that they will follow. You may not notice it right away, but they do notice you, and they remember what they see.

People don't light a lamp and put it under a basket but on a lamp stand, and it gives light to everyone in the house. In the same way, let your light shine before people in such a way that they will see your good actions and glorify your Father in heaven.[90]

As we become more intentionally aware of opportunities to show we CARE, we will be moved more quickly to action. Over time, this action will become a lifestyle, shown not so much by what we do as who we are. As we grow to see the world differently, the world will also see us differently. They will see how we are spending our currencies of time, influence, and love.

The people with whom we come into contact will have a choice to make. They will either join us, continue to observe us at a distance, or write us off as fools. In any case, our actions will be noticed. In a "me first" culture, someone who puts others first will stand out. Someone observing that might be moved to pay it forward, or they might feel convicted because they aren't doing that. Some people might be moved from jealousy to anger if they see someone else getting help that they think they deserve. You don't usually know how people will react when you step out in faith like this. Nevertheless, it is imperative that we do not let fear crowd out our faith, because fear gets nothing done. Faith glorifies God, and God honors faith. This journey is yours. Its value does not depend upon the opinions of the people who have chosen not to walk alongside you. To lead a fulfilling life, and ultimately a *fulfilled* life, you will have to train yourself to listen to the people who are headed in the same direction as you.

All of us have no cloth over our faces. People can see that we have some of the bright and wonderful light that the Lord has. And we are becoming brighter and brighter, more and more like him. It is the Lord, the Spirit, who does this.[91]

We need to cultivate a mindset of not needing to see the results of our actions right away. "Cultivate" is an appropriate word to use, because in a way, we're like farmers. A farmer plants the seed and tends the field, but the farmer does not control the sun and the rain. He can help his crop to grow better, perhaps, but he is not the one who makes it grow. But we are different from farmers in that we are not responsible for harvesting the crop.

It can be challenging to accept that truth in the face of a culture that demands *evidence*. The world needs to see to believe. Until you unlearn that thought process, you will have a very difficult time understanding that you really are making a difference by showing you CARE. A skeptic will see, then believe (maybe), *then* act. To live your calling effectively, however, first you must believe in your cause and then act upon that belief. Only after you have acted will you see, and even then, maybe not right away.

As a farmer plants his crop, trusting that it will grow, so we must also trust that living our calling will produce results. Discipline and steady plodding lead to personal transformation and, by extension, world change. No one ever ran a marathon in ten seconds. Then again, if it only took ten seconds to run a marathon, more people would do it. The important thing is to keep running, because unlike a literal marathon, where we know the finish line is in 26.2 miles, we don't know where the finish line of our life is going to be.

Your life will not be perfect just because you have decided to find and live your calling, but as you keep your purpose in front of you, staying focused on the needs of others around you, what you will find is that your own personal problems become less significant to you. They don't go away, but they don't bother you as much as they otherwise would, because you have something greater than your troubles upon which to focus your attention.

> *If you do things the same way you've always done them, you'll get the same outcomes you've always gotten. In order to change your outcomes, you've got to do things differently.*[92]

Ultimately, if you want your life to be different, then you have to live your life differently. It's not enough to want results without working toward them, because you can't go somewhere else by standing still. It's not enough to pray for guidance without acting on God's answer when it comes. As James wrote, *"Faith without works is dead."*[93]

Three small words: 'God bless you'

A good way to develop the habit of doing things differently is to start with small things, subtle changes in your routine that are out of your comfort zone, yet easy to do. I have a friend who, to my amazement, says that my habit of adding a few words to my daily routine is one he emulated with noticeable results:

"I noticed that in Jimmy's encounters with people he knew and with people he had never met before, Jimmy would freely—and with earnest conviction—tell people "God bless you." Jimmy's from the South, but this was clearly no act of Southern courtesy. By his words and the way he said them, he was truly wishing God's blessing upon those folks that he encountered.

"So, in my attempt to be more godly, I vowed I'd do the same, and I'd do so with conviction and sincerity. It went well. People seemed to like hearing "God bless you," and it soon became easier for me to say it. I suppose I had a little sinful and prideful attitude of, "Hey, God, look at me. I'm telling people that I hope you bless them!"

"Then there came the phone call with Jimmy that rattled my cage. At that end of the call when he routinely gave me those encouraging words, "God bless you," Jimmy instead said, "John, I love you, brother."
"I was raised in a family in which it was always assumed that our parents loved us children and that we children loved our parents, but those words of love were never spoken. It was not until I was well into middle age that I ever told my parents that I 'loved' them, and they quickly responded that they 'loved' me. I then continued on with my life, assuming no one would ever hear the words "I love you" from me other than my wife, my own children and grandchildren, plus this later-in-life addition of my parents.

"I realized what had just happened in this phone call when Jimmy told me that he loved me—and I didn't like it. God had used Jimmy to get me to verbalize more freely my love for the important people in my life, and maybe to an even larger circle. And that was far more than just my parents, wife, children, and grandchildren. It was one thing to tell the people in my life 'God bless you,' but saying to them 'I love you' was a whole different situation. I wasn't sure I wanted to do that, or that I *could* do that.

"I started out slowly at first. I was embarrassed at times as I started saying this to my extended family and to my Christian friends, and even to a few acquaintances. I wondered if the folks I said it to shared my embarrassment, as I expressed that I did, indeed, love them. It's still a work in progress, and there remains a large number of people that I feel convicted by God's Spirit to let them know that I do truly love them. I have no doubt that it is what God would have me do because in this little expression of 'I love you,' it is a statement, in my belief, that God loves them."

Finish strong

Because we are creatures of habit who thrive upon comfort, our tendency when we introduce something new into our lives is to "work it into our schedule." But if you are squeezing something new into your scheduling, then you are essentially assigning that new task or event a lower priority than what you are already doing. You didn't change what you were already doing; you just added to it. At best, you will subconsciously have the attitude that you will get to this new thing if and when you have time. But during stressful weeks when you just don't have enough time to get it all done, what becomes the casualty? That's right, the new thing. When we are under pressure, we fall back to our routine to restore our sense of balance and comfort.

So obviously, if we're going to do something new in our lives, we're going to have to do it in a new way as well. Instead of trying in vain to prioritize our schedule, we need to look at it from the viewpoint of scheduling our priorities. Stephen Covey, author of *The 7 Habits of Highly Effective People*, calls this "choosing the big rocks." If you have identified some things it's important to change in your life, begin your scheduling around those things and let the less important things be the ones to fall by the wayside, if something must. You might find after a short while that you don't really miss the things you've stopped doing as you begin the journey of living your calling.

No, dear brothers and sisters, I have not achieved it, but I focus on this one thing: Forgetting the past and looking forward to what lies ahead, I press on to reach the end of the race and receive the heavenly prize for which God, through Christ Jesus, is calling us.[94]

Dear reader, this is the first day of the rest of your life. I genuinely wish you well on this journey. It might be a little unnerving at first to try to live life in a totally new way, but it's exciting as well. Keep your eyes fixed on your calling, your heart set on the well-being of others, your hands busy, and your feet in motion. Take notes on your journey so you can look back at them years from now and see how far you've come. Trust me, this will all be worth it.

And God bless you.

Thought Conditioners

For more than thirty years, I have been collecting what I like to refer to as "Thought Conditioners." I found that these quick sayings not only helped me form some of my own beliefs or ideas, but that sharing them also helped others in various situations over the years.

These sayings are from mentors, great speakers or books that I've enjoyed reading. Here is a sample of my "Thought Conditioners" that I hope will help you on your journey.
Blessings,

Jimmy Rousey

Don't let the permanent be sacrificed on the altar of the immediate.

The world measures how big a person is by height;
God measures a person by how far they are willing to bend down.

You are either green and growing or ripe and rotting.

Plan your work, work your plan.

The more you learn, the more you earn.

Leadership is doing the right things for the right reasons with the right ATTITUDE.

A rut is a grave with both ends knocked out.

"One of these days" means none of these days.

Though I cannot go back again, my friend, anyone can start from now and make a brand new end.

Friends are like elevator buttons—they can take you up or down.

Doesn't matter what your status in life is—when you cut yourself you bleed.

To keep up I can't let up.

Pigs get fat. Hogs get slaughtered.

The secret to success is in your daily agenda.

The older I get the better I was.

To the world you might be just one person, but to one person you just might be the world.

Yesterday is like a cancelled check. Tomorrow is like a promissory note. Today is like ready cash—use it wisely, for today is the most precious possession you can have.

You can employ men and hire hands to work for you, but you must win their hearts to have them work with you.
— Wm. J. H. Boetcker

An ounce of loyalty is worth a pound of cleverness.
— Elbert Hubbard

I have often regretted my speech, but never my silence.
— Xenocrates

You make a living by what you get; you make a life by what you give. — Winston Churchill

Excellence is the habit of doing a thousand little things well.

And the trouble is, if you don't risk anything, you risk even more.
— Erica Jong

If you see a bandwagon, it's too late. — Sir James Goldsmith

Remember the banana—when it left the bunch it got skinned.

Heaven, not earth, is my home.

As surely as the compass follows north, your heart will follow your treasure.

Giving isn't a luxury of the rich. It's a privilege of the poor.

God owns everything. I'm His money manager.

Life can be measured by the number of breaths that one takes, and some of those moments are breathtaking.

Feedback is the Breakfast of Champions.

Pain must be my *friend*.

Where God guides, God provides. — Jerry Quick

What is happiness? Happiness is not having what you want, it is wanting what you have.

What is success? Finding your purpose or mission in life and fulfilling it.

What is love? Giving of one's self to another and expecting nothing in return.

Words may show a man's wit, but actions show his meaning. — Benjamin Franklin

It only takes a moment to be kind, but the results can last a lifetime.

Kindness is a language we all understand—even the blind can see it and the deaf can hear it. — Mother Teresa

So many things to think about, so little to worry about.

Happy moments, praise God;
difficult moments, seek God;
quiet moments, worship God;
painful moments, trust God;
every moment, thank God.

GOLF: Game of Life First.

A man stands his tallest when he is down on his knees.

Old men plant trees they never plan to sit under.

Forgiveness does not change the past, but it does enlarge the future. — Paul Beose

If you really want to humble someone, ask them how is their prayer life. — Martin Luther

Bloom where you are planted. — Mary Engelbreit

What is on the throne of your heart?

How would you live your life, absent all reward and all punishment?

Do your givin' while you are livin', cause you're-a-knowin' where it's-a-goin'.

If everyone followed Christ the way that I follow Christ, what would the world look like?

If nothing changes—nothing changes.

I am created—He the Creator;
I am a sinner—He is the Savior.

Humility is not thinking less of yourself,
it is thinking about yourself less.

African saying: If you want to go fast, go alone; if you want to go far, go together.

At the end of the day, you have to sleep with yourself. (Conscience.)

You ride the horse that got you there. (Habits.)

If it doesn't fit, don't force it—you will not only ruin the part but the tool. (Also applies to people.)

The employee you have after six months is the employee you deserve.

Very few people really change after twenty-five years.

Do it right the first time, even when you feel like you don't have time, because you will make time to do it over when you definitely will not have the time.

Work hard, don't take it hard.

Wickedness is the opposite of trust.

The brief shall be heard again!

Faith glorifies God and God glorifies faith.

Funny how falling feels like flying for awhile.

Too often we judge others by their actions and judge ourselves by our best intentions. — President George W. Bush

Don't confuse motion with progress or progress with results.

When a man is wrapped up in himself, he makes a pretty small package. — John Ruskin

Knowledge is acquiring; wisdom is getting rid of stuff.

EGO: Edging God Out.

A good sermon or speech has a good beginning, a good ending and not much in between.

What matters most in the end matters most now!

J- Jesus first
O- Others second
Y- Yourself last

B- Being
U- Under
S- Satan's
Y- Yoke

CHAPTER 1 DISCUSSION QUESTIONS

1. When you were growing up, what did "success" mean to you? Has your definition of success changed over time?
2. Can you think of a time in your life when you were motivated to make a name for yourself? How did it turn out?
3. What are you passionate about?
4. What is something you have done in your life that really made you feel good about yourself? Did you ever do that thing again?
5. If you could have a do-over with your life up to this point, what would you change, if anything? Why?
6. What is something you can say or do for younger generations to help "stop the erosion?"
7. Do you regularly make time in your life to do the things that you CARE about most? If not, what has stopped you?
8. If someone looked at how you spend your time and money, what would they say that you CARE about?
9. When was the last time you showed how much you CARE to someone without expecting anything in return?
10. Of the "Four T's" (time, talent, treasure, and touch), which is the easiest for you to give? Which is most challenging?

CHAPTER 2 DISCUSSION QUESTIONS

1. What is the first thing that comes to mind when you hear the word "calling?"
2. What is something you have wasted money on?
3. What did you consider a waste of time when you were growing up? Has your perspective changed on that?
4. What do you currently waste the most time on?
5. When was the last time you complained about not having enough time to do something? What was keeping you from doing that thing?
6. What would you say is on your "throne" today?
7. What is one distraction that you could remove from your life right now and not miss it?

8. Which of your possessions would be hardest to give up?

9. Have you had a time in your life where you have had to let go of a "Norman Rockwell picture" of how you thought life should be? How did it turn out?

10. Has there been an activity or cause in your life that you thought might be your calling but turned out not to be? If so, how and when did you realize that it wasn't?

11. What is something that you would spend time doing regularly even if you didn't get paid for doing it?

12. What is something in your life that you have resisted doing, but after doing it, wished you had done it sooner?

13. Has anyone ever told you that you've "missed your calling?" To what were they referring?

14. What do you sense God is prompting you to do with the time and resources that you have available? Did His answer surprise you?

CHAPTER 3 DISCUSSION QUESTIONS

1. Who are some people who shaped your worldview into what it is today, for better or for worse?

2. What are some ways that you have found yourself "becoming your parents?" If you have children, what are some things you have seen in their behavior that you know they learned from you?

3. What is more important to you when you are being served as a customer: accuracy or a good attitude?

4. How does it make you feel when you encounter someone whose actions do not match his or her words?

5. Have you ever been around someone whose negative attitude ruined everyone else's day? Have you ever been that person?

6. Can you think of a difficult time in your life that ended up working out for the better in the long run?

7. Can you name a person in your life who can help you check your attitude?

8. Can you think of a time when you got what you wanted but

were still not happy?

9. What is the one thing you want most to be remembered for after you're gone? Why?

10. What do you believe you really deserve in life?

11. Have you ever been put in charge of somebody else's possessions? Did you treat those things differently than your own?

12. Do you ever feel overwhelmed by the problems of the world? If so, how did you overcome that?

13. Are you task-oriented or people-oriented?

14. What is something you can do today that will make someone else's life easier?

15. Is there a grudge that you have been holding that you need to get rid of today?

CHAPTER 4 DISCUSSION QUESTIONS

1. Can you think of a relationship in your life when your *primary* motivation was to see what you could get out of it?

2. If you're married or have been married, what is an adjustment you had to make to the expectations you had going into the marriage? (If you're not married, what expectations do you think you might have of a future spouse that could potentially cause conflict?)

3. Does the idea that you are working for the Lord change your perspective on how you go about your daily work?

4. Who is the first person that comes to mind when you think about somebody you respect? What is special about that person?

5. Think of a time when someone has lied to you. What did it take for that person to earn back your respect, if indeed he or she has?

6. Have you ever told a lie specifically to avoid an uncomfortable situation? What was the result?

7. Can you think of a time recently when you were not "being present?" Did you catch yourself, or did someone else point it out to you?

8. Have you ever been in a situation where you had to receive assistance from someone you didn't like? How did that make you feel?

9. Have you ever found yourself in a position where you were able to assist someone against whom you were prejudiced in some way? What did you do?

10. Have you struggled in your life with holding grudges? If so, what's one grudge you can let go of today?

CHAPTER 5 DISCUSSION QUESTIONS

1. Have you ever felt underappreciated at work? Did this feeling affect your performance? If so, how?

2. Who has been an example of excellence in your life?

3. Can you remember the first time you gave your very best at something without a promise of a reward? Did you find it easier or harder to do your best at that activity, knowing that you might not even be recognized for your efforts?

4. When was the last time someone had an opportunity to encourage you when you needed it, but failed to do so? How did you react?

5. Can you recall some words of encouragement spoken to you in your past that still affect you today? Have you ever thanked the person who said them to you?

6. Can you think of a way you have put your personal signature on a job and made it uniquely your own?

7. Are you a perfectionist? If so, do you see that as a good or bad thing?

8. Can you think of something that you never started because you were afraid you would fail? Looking back on that, do you feel that your fear was justified?

9. Are there any unnecessary tasks that you can cross off your to-do list this week in order to make yourself more effective?

10. What are some "fishhooks" you need to avoid in your life to keep your eyes fixed on your goal?

11. Can you think of a time recently when you were surprised by somebody going above and beyond for you?

Bibliography

CHAPTER 1

[1] Proverbs 12:15 *World English Bible by Public Domain. The name "World English Bible" is trademarked. (WEB)*

[2] Proverbs 15:22 *Holy Bible, New International Version®, NIV® Copyright © 1973, 1978, 1984, 2011 by Biblica, Inc.® (NIV)*

[3] Half, R. (n.d.). *BrainyQuote.com. (Xplore Inc., 2013) Retrieved July 31, 2013, from* http://www.brainyquote.com/quotes/quotes/r/roberthalf384464.html

[4] Philippians 2:12-13 J. B. Phillips, *"The New Testament in Modern English", 1962 edition by HarperCollins (PHILLIPS)*

[5] *Charisma News U.S. (2012, October 21). Retrieved August 14, 2013, from Charisma News:* http://www.charismanews.com/us/34357-rick-warrens-the-purpose-driven-life-celebrates-10-years

[6] 1 Corinthians 7:30-31 *Easy-to-Read Version Copyright © 2006 by World Bible Translation Center (ERV)*

[7] 1 Timothy 6:17-19 *Contemporary English Version Copyright © 1995 by American Bible Society (CEV)*

[8] Deuteronomy 4:9 *The Voice Bible Copyright © 2012 Thomas Nelson, Inc. The Voice™ translation © 2012 Ecclesia Bible Society All rights reserved. (VOICE)*

[9] James 2:15-17 *Common English Bible Copyright © 2011 by Common English Bible (CEB)*

[10] Copyright © 2009 Zondervan

[11] Matthew 6:19-21 *Complete Jewish Bible Copyright © 1998 by David H. Stern. All rights reserved. (CJB)*

[12] 1 John 2: 15-17 *Holy Bible. New Living Translation Copyright © 1996, 2004, 2007 by Tyndale House Foundation. Used by permission of Tyndale House Publishers Inc., Carol Stream, Illinois 60188. All rights reserved. (NLT)*

[13] *If Nothing Changes, Nothing Changes Copyright ©1986 by Earnie Larsen. International Marriage Encounter*

14 Rice, Christopher M. (2000). Life Means So Much. On *Smell the Color 9*. Nashville, Tennessee: Rocketown Records.

15 Rubin, Gretchen (2009). *The Happiness Project: Or Why I Spent a Year Trying to Sing in the Morning, Clean My Closets, Fight Right, Read Aristotle, and Generally Have More Fun. Retrieved from* http://www.goodreads.com/quotes/239043-the-days-are-long-but-the-years-are-short

16 Zaillian, Steven (Screenwriter) (1993) *Schindler's List*

17 Huxley, Aldous (1958) *Brave New World Revisited. New York, NY: Harper & Brothers*

18 https://newsroom.fb.com/company-info/ retrieved July 15, 2017

19 Woollaston, Victoria (2013, October 8) *How often do you check your phone? The average person does it 110 times a DAY (and up to every 6 seconds in the evening). Daily Mail. Retrieved January 16, 2015 from* http://www.dailymail.co.uk/sciencetech/article-2449632/How-check-phone-The-average-person-does-110-times-DAY-6-seconds-evening.html

20 Murray, B. [BillMurray]. (2013, May 12). Phones get thinner and smarter. People get fatter and more stupid. [Tweet]. Retrieved from https://twitter.com/billmurray

21 (2014, February 17) *Viewers prefer TV sets over mobile devices. BBC Retrieved February 23, 2014 from* http://www.bbc.co.uk/news/business-26221364

22 *How Much Do You Know About Video Games? Entertainment Software Rating Board. Retrieved February 23, 2014 from* http://www.esrb.org/about/video-game-industry-statistics.jsp

23 (2011, January 13) *Average Time Spent Online per U.S. Visitor in 2010. comScore Data Mine. Retrieved February 23, 2014 from* http://www.comscoredatamine.com/2011/01/average-time-spent-on-line-per-u-s-visitor-in-2010/?hstc=178552891.1c4621a536b0513e9af5a76fd7aeabb0.1393214116332.1393214116332.13932141163321&hssc=178552891.1.1393214116333& hsfp=2407978477

24 Wilson, Chris (2014, January 27). *How Much Time Have You Wasted on Facebook? TIME Tech. Retrieved February 23, 2014 from* http://techland.time.com/2014/01/27/how-much-time-have-you-

wasted-on-facebook/# 25 Giglio, Louie. (2006). *Wired for a Life of Worship.* Retrieved from http://worship.com/2007/03/louie-giglio-wired-for-a-life-of-worship-part-1/

26 Proverbs 3:5-6 (VOICE)

27 Luke 2:49 (ERV)

28 2 Peter 1:10-11 (NIV)

29 Churchill, Winston. (1874-1965). Quoted October 10, 1908, at Kinnaird Hall, Dundee, Scotland

30 Ephesians 2:10 *The Living Bible Copyright © 1971 by Tyndale House Foundation. Used by permission of Tyndale House Publishers Inc., Carol Stream, Illinois 60188. All rights reserved. (TLB)*

31 1 Corinthians 13:12 (VOICE)

32 James 1:22-24 (PHILLIPS)

33 Blackaby, Henry & Richard and King, Claude (1990). *Experiencing God: Knowing and Doing the Will of God.*

Retrieved from http://www.parsonsuniverse.com/bmiweb/eg_Sample.pdf

34 James 1:5-8. *(TLB)*

CHAPTER 3

35 Hebrews 12:1a *The Message Copyright © 1993, 1994, 1995, 1996, 2000, 2001, 2002 by Eugene H. Peterson.*

36 Kinnaman, David and Gabe Lyons. (2007). *unchristian. Grand Rapids, Michigan: BakerBooks.*

37 Ronsvalle, John L. and Sylvia. (2013). *The State of Church Giving through 2011.* Retrieved from http://www.emptytomb.org/scg-11chap8.pdf

38 Barna, George. (2001). *Growing True Disciples. Colorado Springs, Colorado: WaterBrook Press.*

39 Matthew 5:14-16 (CEV)

40 Jones, Charlie. (1968). *Life is Tremendous. Carol Stream, Illinois: Tyndale House Publishers.*

[41] Havner, V. (n.d.) *BrainyQuote.com.* *(Xplore Inc., 2013) Retrieved January 27, 2015, from* http://www.brainyquote.com

[42] Swindoll, Charles R. (1982). *Strengthening Your Grip. Waco, Texas: Word Books, Inc.*

[43] Wright, Randal. *Priorities. Achieving Your Life Mission. Retrieved from* http://www.achieveyourlifemission.com/quotes

[44] Psalm 24:1 *New English Translation* ® *Copyright* ©1996-2006 by *Biblical Studies Press, L.L.C. (NET)*

[45] Eisely, Loren. (1969). *The Unexpected Universe. San Diego, California: Harcourt, Brace and World.*

[46] Warren, Rick. (2002). *The Purpose-Driven Life. Grand Rapids, Michigan:* Zondervan.

[47] Colossians 3:23-25. (MSG)

[48] 1 Peter 2:21-23 (PHILLIPS)

[49] Philippians 2:3-8 (PHILLIPS)

[50] Formsma, Brad. (2014). *I Like Giving. Colorado Springs, Colorado: WaterBrook Press.*

[51] Hugo, Victor. (1862). *Les Miserables. Brussels: A. Lacroix, Verboeckhoven & Co.*

CHAPTER 4

[52] Colossians 3:22-24 (ERV)

[53] Smith, Jacquelyn. (2013). *How to Get Your Co-Workers to Like You Better. Retrieved February 4, 2015, from* http://www.forbes.com/sites/jacquelynsmith/2013/02/06/how-to-get-your-co-workers-to-like-you-better/

[54] Matthew 20:25-28 (ERV)

[55] Miller, Donald. (2012). *The Devastating Power of Lies in a Relationship. Retrieved February 11, 2015, from* http://storylineblog.com/2012/04/05/the-devastating-power-of-lies-in-a-relationship/

[56] Morgan, Carol. (2014). *You're Here. But You're Not. Retrieved February 11, 2105 from* http://www.huffingtonpost.com/dr-carol-morgan/youre-here-but-youre-not

57 Osteen, J. [JoelOsteen]. (2013, March 7). The greatest gift you can give someone is your time, your attention, your love, your concern. [Tweet]. Retrieved from https://twitter.com/joelosteen

58 1 John 4:19 (CEV)

59 John 3:16. *The Names of God Bible (without notes) Copyright ©* 2011 by Baker Publishing Group. *(NOG)*

60 (2014, December 30) *Relational Repair. Wisdom Hunters. Retrieved December 30, 2014 from* http://www.wisdomhunters.com/relational-repair

61 Matthew 5:23-24 (VOICE)

62 Proverbs 17:9 (NOG)

63 Osgood, Charles. (n.d.) *A Poem About Responsibility. Retrieved February 17, 2015 from* http://www.businessballs.com/inspirational_motivational_quotes

64 Ephesians 6:5-8 *The Holy Bible, English Standard Version Copyright © 2001 by Crossway Bibles, a publishing ministry of Good News Publishers.*

65 Lewis, C.S. Retrieved October 28, 2015 from http://www.qotd.org/search/single.html?qid=47646

66 Malachi 1:6-8 (NLT)

67 Young, Jeffrey S. (1988) *Steve Jobs, the Journey is the Reward. Retrieved from* http://www.amazon.com/Steve- Journey-Reward-Jeffrey-Young/dp/155802378X

68 John 13:15 (PHILLIPS)

69 1 Thessalonians 2:3-7 (PHILLIPS)

70 Psalm 75:6-7 (TLB)

71 Ephesians 4:29b (NLT)

72 Matthew 12:34b (ESV)

73 Hawk, Nelson *Words Rec. 2013. Matt Hammitt, Seth Mosley, Jon Steingard. MP3.*

74 for KING & COUNTRY *Matter Rec. 2014. Luke Smallbone, Joel Smallbone, Seth Mosley. CD*

[75] Molassis, Gus. (2014, December). *"Barbara Glanz—Contagious Enthusiasm." Scene, 100-107. Retrieved from* http://issuu.com/scene_magazine

[76] Ibid

[77] Shah, Murad S. Retrieved December 9, 2015 from https://www.goodreads.com/author/show/7868471.Murad_S_Shah

[78] Carlson, Chuck. (2004) *Game of My Life: 25 Stories of Packers Football. Retrieved from* https://en.wikiquote.org/wiki/Vince_Lombardi

[79] Seacrest, Ryan. Retrieved December 9, 2015 from http://www.brainyquote.com/quotes

[80] Exodus 3:11-12, 4:1-4, 10-12 (NIV)

[81] Drucker, Peter F. (1967) *The Effective Executive. Retrieved from* http://www.brainyquote.com/quotes

[82] Ibid

[83] Galatians 6:9-10a (ERV)

[84] 2 Timothy 4: 5-8. (CJB)

[85] Matthew 5:41. (PHILLIPS)

[86] Kroc, R. & Anderson, R. (1977). *Grinding It Out: The Making of McDonald's.*

[87] James 1:12 (VOICE)

[88] Proverbs 29:7 *New American Bible, revised edition. Copyright © 2010, 1991, 1986, 1970 by Confraternity of Christian Doctrine, Inc. (NABRE)*

[89] Braude, Jacob M. & Van Ekeren, Glenn (Rev.). (1991). *Braude's Treasury of Wit & Humor for All Occasions.*

Retrieved from http://www.goodreads.com/book/show/10819909-braude-s-treasury-of-wit-humor-for-all-occasions

[90] Matthew 5:15-16. *International Standard Version. Copyright © 1995-2014 by ISV Foundation. (ISV)*

[91] 2 Corinthians 3:18. *Worldwide English (New Testament)© 1969, 1971, 1996, 1998 by SOON Educational Publications (WE)*

92 Hansen, M. V. (2002). *Favorite Quotes from Jack Canfield and Mark Victor Hansen. Retrieved from* http://downloads.chickensoup.com/file/Jack_and_Mark_Quotes.pdf

93 James 2:26b (NABRE)

94 Philippians 3:13-14 (NLT)

Thank You

I am so grateful for all the mentors, friends, family, partners, teachers, pastors and associates who have influenced me and help shape my journey here on earth by providing love, wisdom, accountability and joy. In a very large way each of you have made a direct contribution to this book being written.

Thank you to Una, Loyd, Greatmother, Mom, Dad, Tracy, Lori, Alex, Neal, Granny, Kris, Chris, Jess, Max, Coy, Glenn, Tim, Tom, Randy, Doug, David, Ted, Mike, Dan, Daniel, Diane, Julio, Eric, Al, David, Bryan, Brian, Boyd, Howard, Pete, Joe, John, Lawrence, Jack, Bob, Dwight, Shay, Dirk, TC, Angela, Bill, Mark, Dennis, Chip, Jane, Jennifer, June, Tamiko, Cathy, Jeff, Jerry, Aunts, Uncles, Bruce, Debbie, Sandy, Wayne, JoAnn, Scottie, Ray, Charlie, Jake, Bobby, Kevin, Cindy, Peter, Ben, Wes, Chas, Jon, Stanley, Larry, Scott, Emma, Betty, Thomas, Todd, Jan, Rose, Terri, Larry, Danny, Becky, Paula, Kathy, Casey, Steele, Julie and Joseph, Dale, Barry, Tommy, Matt, Wes, and Chas.

My sincere appreciation to Scott, Emma, Megan, Candice and Peter who worked with me to get the book completed.

Many years ago, a very wise man told me it is not the words that are spoken that are important, it is the meaning behind the words. With that in mind, I simply say to all, and especially my wife, thank you, and I love you each and every one.

I'd like to invite you to learn more about Our Family of Companies, headquartered in my hometown of Stanford, Kentucky.

Learn more about Our Family of Companies below:

First Southern National Bank
www.fsnb.net

UTG
www.utgins.com

Kentucky Soaps and Such
www.kentuckysoapsandsuch.com

The Bluebird
www.bluebirdnatural.com

Wilderness Road Guest Houses & Rooms
new.wildernessroadguest.com

Made in the USA
Middletown, DE
18 June 2018